SEP 13 2011

D0438003

Civil Liberties in China

The *Understanding China Today* series offers students and general readers the opportunity to thoroughly examine and better understand the key contemporary issues that continue to keep China in the news and sometimes at the center of global controversy. These issues include business, technology, politics, government, civil liberties, family life, and gender concerns, among others.

Narrative chapters in each volume provide an introduction and brief history of the topic, followed by comprehensive discussions of the subject area as it pertains to China's present and future. With each volume, specialists and scholars present a solid, up-to-date foundation for learning about contemporary China, written in an accessible, engaging manner.

As the world moves into the second decade of the 21st century, China's position on the global stage is more prominent than ever. The *Understanding China Today* series provides vital insight into this international powerhouse for new generations of students and others seeking to understand a complex, ever-changing nation with a future as fascinating as its past.

Civil Liberties in China

XIAOBING LI

3 1336 08888 2114

UNDERSTANDING CHINA TODAY

ABC-CLIO

Santa Barbara, California • Denver, Colorado • Oxford, England

Library of Congress Cataloging-in-Publication Data

Li, Xiaobing, 1954-
Civil liberties in China / Xiaobing Li.
p. cm. — (Understanding China today)
Includes bibliographical references and index.
ISBN 978-0-313-35895-1 (hard copy: alk. paper) — ISBN 978-0-313-35896-8
(e-book) 1. Civil rights—China. I. Title.
JC599.C6L56   2010
323.0951—dc22   2010031545

ISBN: 978-0-313-35895-1
EISBN: 978-0-313-35896-8

14   13   12   11   10   1   2   3   4   5

This book is also available on the World Wide Web as an eBook.
Visit www.abc-clio.com for details.

ABC-CLIO, LLC
130 Cremona Drive, P.O. Box 1911
Santa Barbara, California 93116-1911

This book is printed on acid-free paper ∞

Manufactured in the United States of America

Contents

Acknowledgments

Many people at the University of Central Oklahoma (UCO) have contributed to this book and deserve recognition. First, I would like to thank Provost William (Bill) J. Radke, Vice Provost Patricia A. LaGrow, Dean of the College of Liberal Arts Pamela Washington, Dean of the Jackson College of Graduate Studies Richard Bernard, and Associate Dean of the College of Liberal Arts Gary Steward. They have been very supportive of the project over the past four years. The faculty merit-credit program sponsored by the Office of Academic Affairs and Liberal Arts College research grant at UCO provided funding for my research and student assistants.

I wish to thank my Chinese colleagues and collaborators at the Chinese Academy of Social Sciences, China Society for Strategy and Management Research, Peking University, East China Normal University, and Southwest University of Political Science and Law. I am grateful to Dai Chaowu, Niu Jun, Wan Qing, Yang Kuisong, and Zhang Pengfei for their help and advice on my research in China.

Special thanks go to Professor Yonglin Jiang of Bryn Mawr College in Pennsylvania, who proofread the entire manuscript. UCO professor Kenny L. Brown also proofread and critically reviewed several chapters. Professors Keith Rollin Eakins, Randy J. Jones, and Jessica Sheetz-Nguyen at UCO made important suggestions on the research, outline, and early draft. Jeffery Widener reproduced the map.

Candace Carollo provided secretarial assistance. Lacey D. Bryant helped with document processing. Several graduate and undergraduate students at UCO contributed to the book, including Hugh Long, Michael Molina, Xiaowei Wang, and Yang Yu. I also wish to thank Kaitlin Ciarmiello, acquisitions editor at ABC-CLIO, who patiently guided the editing of the book. Any remaining errors of facts, language usage, and interpretation are my own.

List of Abbreviations

ACFTU	All-China Federation of Trade Unions
ACWF	All-China Women's Federation
CCP	Chinese Communist Party
CCYL	Chinese Communist Youth League
CPG	Central People's Government
CPPCC	Chinese People's Political Consultative Conference
FCCC	Foreign Correspondent's Club of China
GAPP	General Administration of Press and Publications
GMD	Guomindang (Chinese Nationalist Party)
NPC	National People's Congress
OHCHR	Office of the High Commissioner for Human Rights (United Nations)
PAP	People's Armed Police
PLA	People's Liberation Army
PRC	People's Republic of China
RFA	Radio Free Asia
RMB	*Renminbi* (Chinese currency)
ROC	Republic of China
RTL	Reeducation Through Labor
SARS	Severe Acute Respiratory Syndrome
TAR	Tibet Autonomous Region
WTO	World Trade Organization
XUAR	Xinjiang Uyghur Autonomous Region

Note on Transliteration

The *hanyu pinyin* romanization system is applied to Chinese names of persons, places, and terms. The transliteration is also used for the titles of Chinese publications. Names of individuals are written in the Chinese way, surname first, such as Mao Zedong. Some popular names have traditional Wade-Giles spellings appearing in parentheses after the first use of the *hanyu pinyin*, such as Jiang Jieshi (Chiang Kai-shek) and Sun Zhongshan (Sun Yat-sen), as do popular names of places like the Changjiang (Yangtze River) and Huanghe (Yellow River). The order is reversed for a very few places whose names are widely known, such as Tibet (Xizang) and Peking (Beijing) University.

Introduction: Progress and Problems

Chinese civil liberties, often different from those in Western countries, are usually a controversial topic on the international stage. Many Americans and peoples of other nations are concerned about China's dreadful record on civil and human rights. These problems will be difficult to fix quickly, because they have larger implications for Chinese society and government as a whole. To understand Chinese law and order, and therefore to be able to work with China toward international standards, the U.S. government and American schools are dedicating more resources to understand the country's evolving democratization. American policy makers place much emphasis on the development of civil liberties as a step toward transforming China into a democratic society and for changing the relationship between the Chinese people and their government.

President Barack Obama explained the significance of civil liberties in modern society to an audience of young students during his first trip to China, in November 2009. Speaking at a town-hall-style meeting in Shanghai, President Obama stated that the civil liberties and human rights that Americans stand for are not only for the American people. The president told the 300 Chinese college students in attendance: "These freedoms of expression, and worship, of access to information and political participation—we believe they are universal rights. They should be available to all people, including ethnic and religious minorities, whether they are in the United States, China or any nation." When a student asked him about Internet freedom, Obama described himself as a "big supporter of noncensorship" and said that criticism enabled by freedom of expression in the United States made him a better president.[1] The White House, however, was disappointed because the Chinese government refused to broadcast Obama's speech live on national television networks and instead showed it only on a local Shanghai television station. Many human rights groups and China watchers warn that a better understanding of the current situation in China and a better approach to their civil liberty problems have become more important than ever before.

This book examines the current condition of civil liberties in China by explaining the country's legal system and major judicial problems, as well as introducing and exploring the theory and practice of constitutional rights by identifying key issues in Chinese ideology, government, and society and the international environment. The assessment of historical evidence and empirical data in this work puts major legal cases in the context of Chinese traditions, culture, and legal experience. Using comprehensive coverage to create a solid foundation of knowledge, this work provides a better understanding of Chinese political concerns, constitutional issues, and policy behaviors.

This volume also offers an analytical approach to many unanswered questions through new interpretations and different perspectives by using a cross-cultural methodology to show that China acts according to a consistent inner logic in its judicial affairs. It will clarify key Chinese conceptual frameworks to understand previously confusing or neglected subjects and will provide case studies and policy analyses on civil and human liberties in China. Some general patterns are developed in this work as a way of finding meaning in the cultural, sociological, and political structure of drastically different civilizations. These patterns illuminate current problems in government accountability, public voice, rule of law, and political transparency. Finally, this study offers suggestions for future research on this vitally important topic in today's China.

EAST MEETS WEST

China has a different historical experience in the conception and debates of civil liberties than countries in the West. According to the Western view, civil liberties are an essential commonality of human dignity—a concept that originated in the Enlightenment ideals of universalism, rationality, and modernity. *Civil rights* refers to freedom of speech, freedom of religion, freedom of the press, and freedom of assembly and association, as well as rights of the accused. Some of the rights simply require noninterference on the part of the government.

These civil liberties have protected individual rights in Western democratic countries like the United States for centuries. However, some authoritarian regimes in Asia, like the People's Republic of China (PRC), tend to argue that certain rights are at present unrealizable in their societies for historical, cultural, or political reasons. Some Chinese scholars participating in the debate also defend their government's position that certain civil and political rights, such as freedom of the press or of assembly, are luxuries their country cannot afford.

Few areas of China studies pose more difficulties than that of the country's civil liberties, primarily because of the latter's unique relationship to the legitimacy of the nation's Communist authority and possible political transition from an authoritarian regime to a liberal, if not yet a democratic, government. The Chinese Communist Party (CCP) is still the state's dominant political party and controls the executive, legislative, and judicial systems. The first generation of Chinese Communist leaders, who founded the PRC in 1949, developed their own political, economic, and legal institutions based on the totalitarian model provided by the Soviet Union. Since 1978, when the next generation of leadership took over, the PRC has experienced a wave of tremendous change, especially the evolution of the centrally planned Communist economy into one that embraces the free-market system. This successful reform has transformed China from an agricultural country into an industrialized nation, while transforming the PRC's government from a totalitarian system to an authoritarian one.

The shifting nature of the ongoing reform movement, however, retains contradiction, uncertainty, and mixed characteristics of both tradition and modernity. It has brought about three major problems confronting students of Chinese legal practice: contradictory facts and statistics; frequent changes in policy; and the gap between Chinese practices and international standards. These complex problems make understanding Chinese civil liberties very difficult for Westerners. Tracing Chinese practice from traditional philosophies to modern social life helps explain the transient nature of the boundaries between the individual and the state.

The Chinese government's policy toward its people's civil liberties has often been contradictory. On the Chinese New Year's Eve in February 2008, for example, Hu Jintao, president of the PRC, called for "harmony and innovation" within the country and tried to include all the people in his "humanistic society." But in March, his government brutally crushed protests in the streets of Lhasa, the capital of Tibet (Xizang). Many Americans were shocked and confused by the discrepancy between Hu's policy and his behavior, but this inconsistency is quite common in the formation of policy issues and is particularly apparent in legal practice, one of the major components of Chinese civil liberties. The gap between the constitution and reality, between what the government says and what it does, greatly hinders the study and research of the subject.

Contradictory policies are profoundly entrenched in Chinese culture and tradition. The nation has the oldest civilization in East Asia, with a recorded legal history of more than 3,000 years and has the largest population in the world, at 1.3 billion by the end of the twentieth century. Because of China's unique geographic and demographic characteristics, its legal tradition has emphasized social order and centralized state power. According to the ideologies of Confucianism, Buddhism, and Daoism (Taoism), the individual is considered dependent upon the harmony and strength of the group. Thus, the rights of the individual were not emphasized or necessarily protected by the imperial leadership or subsequent governments, who focused instead on the majority group as representative of the individual. Civil liberties were always regarded as relative and set in the context of interpersonal relations based on the family, clan, and centralized imperial structures. The emperors, considered "son of the heaven," usually justified their authoritarian policy as "mandated by heaven" for the common good.[2]

Harmony is a traditional concept derived from Confucianism, an official ideology of classical China. Confucianism, a combination of

Then-vice president Hu Jintao is shown during a meeting at the Pentagon in Washington, D.C., in May 2002. On March 15, 2003, four months after former president Jiang Zemin relinquished the role of Chinese Communist Party secretary, Hu became president of China. (Courtesy of the Department of Defense.)

several ancient lines of thought, is a humanistic philosophy that emphasizes the close ties between humans and nature. It teaches that moral conduct, inner integrity, righteousness, and kindheartedness should be used to create a harmonious society. In Chinese life, one's virtues of decency, loyalty, sincerity, and benevolence, which are taught by parents, grandparents, and relatives, provide the norms for social conduct. Confucian basic political conservatism makes it a controlling ideology used by most subsequent governments in China, Taiwan, and Hong Kong. The Chinese government currently uses this idealized philosophy of the past as a social and political ethos. The balanced nature of Confucianism may help explain its popularity and success in China and East Asia during the past 2,500 years.

Confucianism, however, is different from the modern concept of "rule of law." It emphasizes a social order that includes good family relationships and a moral government. It justified a paternalistic family pattern—the father's rule as the family authority, or the emperor in the political power center—and family members and the people were under an absolute obligation to obey. As "children" of the emperor, the Chinese people observed traditional ideas, ethical codes, suitable relations, and a mutual obligation between the emperor and themselves to serve the empire for their own welfare and protection. An individual might receive some limited freedoms through his or her loyalty to the emperor, trust by the authority, and hard work for the government. Paternalistic rule was dependent on Confucian ethics and was not secured by a system of formal legal and institutional safeguards. "Ruling by man" or "ruling by emperors' law" was a typical Chinese conception from the past that resulted in a social order that allowed the government to focus on a utilitarian society where the sacrifice of a few for the benefit of many could be engrained into the people.

After Great Britain defeated China during the 1840 Opium War, Chinese society was affected by the influence of Western ideas and institutions. In the late nineteenth century, China, for the first time, was significantly exposed to Western democratic ideas. Scholars and intellectuals began to translate and introduce the ideas of "citizenship," "constitution," and "democracy" to the Manchu emperors, and reformers within and outside the court called for political and social change to transform China into a "rich country with a strong military." Strong conservative forces in the Qing (Ch'ing) Dynasty (1644–1911) opposed the Western ideas, however, and many movements such as the 1898 Hundred Day Reform and 1905 Constitutional Movement failed.[3] For the entire twentieth century, the struggles between conservatives and reformers continued, often focusing on modernization as a method of saving China, with some initiating a middle path that combined both "Eastern spirits and Western technology." Tradition, however, continued to collide with change, resulting in numerous rebellions, wars, and revolutions at the cost of millions of lives.

In October 1911, the republican revolution led by Sun Zhongshan (Sun Yat-sen) ended the Qing Dynasty and established the Republic of

China (ROC). The revolutionaries and some warlords joined forces and set up a provisional government at Nanjing, which elected Sun president and inaugurated him on January 1, 1912. As the founding father of the ROC and the Chinese Nationalist Party (the Guomindang [GMD] or Kuomintang [KMT]), Sun mobilized the masses for the revolution with his "Three Principles of the People": nationalism (both anti-Manchu and anti-imperialist), democracy (a constitution with people's rights), and "people's livelihood" (a classic term for social equality). These three principles included many of the key concepts contained in updated Western ideas.[4] Before a formal constitution was drawn up, the ROC National Assembly enacted a provisional constitution, promulgated on March 11. It stipulated that the ROC was of the people, by the people, and for the people and that all citizens were equal before the law regardless of race, class, or creed.

The 1911 republican revolution, however, failed to turn China into a truly independent and democratic country. The revolutionary leaders lacked an agrarian program that reflected the interests of peasants, who formed a majority of the Chinese. Even though the revolution was incomplete, the struggle for democracy and modernization continued. New ideas from Western civilizations continued to inspire Chinese intellectuals and students, who launched the New Cultural movement in the 1910s and the May 4 Movement of 1919. Western democracy and liberalism began to take root in China during these years.

Most Chinese Communist leaders also studied Western philosophy and ideas. Mao Zedong (Mao Tse-tung), founding member of the CCP and the founding father of the PRC, read Western liberal works by Montesquieu, Thomas Carlyle, and John Stuart Mill. As a result, he changed from a Confucian reformer to a radical liberalist in the late 1910s.[5] Among Western ideologies, Karl Marx, a German philosopher of the nineteenth century, used communism to criticize the predominant Western, capitalist, economic system. Furthermore, he advocated a political system that abolished private ownership of property and created public ownership of the means of production, resulting in an economic and social equality in which distribution and consumption would be based on the common possession of goods and a communal way of life. Marxism emphasized the common will and good of the working, or proletarian, class and seemed to make sense to Chinese radicals like Mao.

The Russian October Revolution of 1917, under the leadership of Vladimir Lenin, provided a model for the Chinese to follow. Lenin attempted to turn Marx's ideas into a reality through a bloody revolution and established the first Communist state, the Soviet Union. The Soviet system, however, was not a Western, republican, or democratic institution. Leninism proved that the Communist movement required the working class to create an uprising in order to gain control of state power that could then be placed under the control of professional revolutionaries.

Mao was drawn to Marxism-Leninism and the Russian experience and became a Marxist-Leninist revolutionary, joining with 50 others to found the CCP in 1921. Thereafter, many of the CCP leaders traveled to Russia and spent years studying Soviet political, military, and legal systems. The Soviet model seemed to work very well for the CCP to survive the GMD military suppression led by Jiang Jieshi (Chiang Kai-shek), president of the ROC, against the Communist movement in 1932–1935.

As Moscow suggested, Mao Zedong established a political coalition with Jiang's GMD during China's war against Japan's invasion from 1937 to 1945. Mao's successful strategy of cooperating with Jiang and mobilizing guerrilla warfare behind Japanese lines increased CCP membership from 40,000 in 1937 to 1.2 million—leading more than a million regular troops and two million militia—by the end of World War II in 1945. Their successful experience convinced Chinese Communist leaders such as Mao that a new China would follow the Soviet model after the CCP took over the country.

The CCP challenged the legitimacy of the Nationalist ROC government and fought the Chinese civil war against the GMD in 1946–1949. Both parties used the ideas of civil liberties and people's rights to mobilize the masses and promote their own political goals. Jiang Jieshi adopted the Constitution of the Republic of China on December 25, 1947, but too late for him to save the mainland China from the Communist takeover. After the CCP's armed forces defeated Jiang's military and won the conflict, Mao Zedong proclaimed the birth of the new Communist state in Beijing in October 1949. Jiang removed the seat of his government from the mainland to Taiwan, where, from 1949 to 1987, the ROC enforced martial law. Taiwan did not hold an election until the 1990s. In mainland China, the

Communist government did not create a constitution until 1954 and had no free elections through the rest of the century.

In the early twenty-first century, the Chinese government continues its struggles between Eastern traditions and Western ideas. Beijing faces the dilemma of protecting Chinese civilization and historic ideologies while using Western ideas and methods to solve new problems created by industrialization and modernization. Beijing chose a middle course that balanced and connected tradition with modernization: a capitalist economy with Communist politics and a liberal society with an authoritarian government. The struggle for a balanced policy has resulted in contradictions and even confrontation in policy making. The government hopes that eventually the apparent opposites will penetrate each other and become part of a final unity—a vision that merely shows an uncertain and unpredictable future.

THE INDIVIDUAL VERSUS THE STATE

The second problem in the Chinese judicial system is the frequent change and deviation in government policy and legal practice, which may be one of the most noticeable phenomena in the operation of China's legal system today. Three elements drive these recurrent shifts in judicial policy construction. The first is that, in order to achieve a balance between traditional normative methods and Western essential elements, policy must frequently realign to cover both sides. The second is a historical reason: that a real legal system, with judicial independence, is still under construction. The CCP is reluctant to tolerate any significant diminution of its authority, and thus the Party Center continues to use the law as an instrument to hold unchecked power rather than creating a regime that protects citizens' rights. The third element is the identity crisis that Chinese Communists faced when they shifted from the Soviet-style state to a socialist state with Chinese characteristics.

What is China now? Is it a Communist, a liberal socialist, or an authoritarian state? This confusion in identity and definition has left many unresolved issues and requires many adjustments, modifications, and corrections in government policy and legal practice. When Mao established the PRC in 1949, he made it clear that China would be a Communist state, and he favored the Soviet Union in the bipolar

Cold War world. As a result, the United States refused to recognize the PRC and instead maintained diplomatic relations with the ROC on Taiwan. Mao's decision to intervene in the Korean War resulted in a period of mutual hostility between China and the United States. Before signing the Korean Armistice Agreement in 1953, the PRC suffered 1.2 million military casualties. Thereafter, the United States pursued a policy of containment with the PRC by creating a trade embargo and rejecting China's representation in the United Nations.[6]

During the early 1950s, Mao carried out Soviet-style social and economic reforms. The Chinese Communist revolution established a new socioeconomic system based on Soviet Marxism-Leninism, modified to fit the Chinese situation, resulting in Mao Zedong Thought. Mao's social reconstruction used Soviet financial, technological, and military support for reconstruction and economic growth. In 1952, Mao called for a national movement to learn from the Soviet Union under the leadership of Joseph Stalin, and China became the most Soviet-influenced country to maintain its identity within the Communist camp through the 1950s.

In the late 1950s, the international Communist movement experienced its most serious difficulties since World War II. The crisis began in 1956 when the Hungarians and Poles challenged Soviet rule. When the new Soviet leader, Nikita Khrushchev, ordered Russian troops and tanks to suppress the revolts and reinstall Communist control in Hungary and Poland, thousands were killed or imprisoned, and hundreds of thousands fled these two countries. This caused many Communists throughout Eastern Europe to lose confidence in their ideology as a historical force of the future.[7] In East Asia, the Moscow–Beijing coalition, the cornerstone of the Communist international alliance, collapsed in 1958–1959. The great Sino-Soviet polemic debate in 1960–1962 further undermined the ideological foundation of the Communist revolution, with Mao criticizing Khrushchev as a "revisionist" who had betrayed Communists throughout the world.

In retrospect, few events during the Cold War played as important a role in shaping the orientation and essence of the conflict as the Sino-Soviet split. Moscow lost its total control of the international Communist movement, and China began to consider the Soviet Union as more of a threat to the country's security than the United States. Subsequently, Beijing began to form a world alliance to stop

Soviet military expansion by improving its relations with major Western powers—including the United States. The PRC became a member of the United Nations and acquired a seat on the Security Council in 1971. U.S. president Richard Nixon saw an opportunity to improve the relationship with China by ending the trade embargo and made a historic visit to Beijing in February 1972. Taking the Soviet threat as an overriding concern, the Sino-U.S. rapprochement led to a quasi-strategic partnership between the two countries and facilitated an improvement in China's status in the international community. When President Gerald Ford traveled to Beijing in 1975, he agreed to terminate the U.S.–Taiwan mutual security treaty and withdraw U.S. military forces from the island.

Khrushchev's fading leadership in the early 1960s, however, did not slow down the Communist revolutions in the world. Instead, some of the leaders became more radical and eagerly pushed their own agendas to an unprecedented level. Among the new Communist movements was Mao's Great Proletarian Cultural Revolution in the 1960s to prevent "revisionists" from taking over in China. Mao mobilized the masses in a spiritual way and turned young people loose to launch a nationwide, disastrous, prolonged revolution against the leader's own political rivals. The Chinese people paid a terrible price for the Cultural Revolution, and from 1966 to 1976 an estimated 30 to 40 million died. By 1976, when Mao died in Beijing, China was a totalitarian state captivated by his cult of personality.

In 1977, Deng Xiaoping (Deng Hsiao-ping) staged his third comeback as the head of the CCP in a new generation of leadership. Firmly in control of Beijing and having removed the Maoists, he made a historical speech, "Emancipate the Mind," at the Third Plenary Session of the Eleventh CCP Central Committee in 1978. In this speech, Deng made a declaration of unprecedented reform and an opening to the world to bring about the "Four Modernizations" in China.[8] Having moved the nation away from the radical revolution and political struggles led so disastrously by Mao, Deng as the leader of the second generation of the CCP began a new era of dramatic economic reconstruction, naming it the "Second Revolution."

To achieve the nation's economic growth and establish a market economy, Deng emphasized international peace and cooperation, resulting in the establishment of diplomatic relations with the United

States on January 1, 1979. Later that year, he became the first top PRC leader to visit America, holding talks with President Jimmy Carter and signing protocols; unlike Mao, he discussed coalition- and consensus-building. Deng's efforts led to a new relationship between the two countries, resulting in increased trade, education, technology, and cultural exchanges. Later he met presidents Ronald Reagan and George H. W. Bush in Beijing during their state visits to China.

The country's economy grew tremendously from 1978 to 1990 at an annual rate of 7 to 9 percent, and China's gross national product more than quadrupled between 1978 and 2000. This economic growth and the subsequent improvement in the standard of living provided legitimacy for the CCP's maintenance of power. Additionally, increased involvement with the international community and economic reform changed the CCP by making the party more responsive to public opinion and people's rights. Deng's China was no longer a totalitarian state.

As a pragmatist rather than an ideologue, Deng began negotiations with the British government in 1982 to resume sovereignty over Hong Kong and with the Portuguese to secure Macao's return. He developed a theory of "one country, two systems" to apply to these two territories, as well as Taiwan, to secure peaceful national reunification. After many years of negotiations, Hong Kong was returned to China in 1997 and Macao in 1999. Meanwhile, a rapid increase in cross-strait trade, visits, and exchanges, as well as multilevel negotiations, began between Beijing and Taiwan in the 1980s. The West described Deng as a "mountain mover," the chief architect of the Four Modernizations that helped propel China into the modern world. Deng was one of few international leaders to be named *Time* magazine's Man of the Year twice, in 1978 and 1985.

Deng, however, did not leave a clear, long-term plan for the new generation of party leadership after his retirement in 1987. The reform, in his own words, still required China to "cross the river by feeling the stones."[9] Unable to solve the economic and social problems and unwilling to begin political reform, Chinese leaders in the summer of 1989 were challenged by prodemocracy student demonstrators who asked for political reforms across the country and protested against corruption and abuse of power. CCP officials ordered Chinese troops to open fire on the protesting students in Tiananmen Square in Beijing on June 4. The government reported that at least

200 civilians, including many college students, were killed, and the troops also suffered some casualties; the Beijing Red Cross estimated 2,600 deaths.

The Tiananmen Square massacre was a major setback to China's reform movement. Viewed from this perspective, the political crisis in 1989 can be understood as a conflict between the inherent totalitarian tendency of a one-party state and the need to recognize the indispensable roles played by various functional groups in achieving economic growth and modernizing society. After the ensuing massacre, Western countries joined in widespread condemnation of the event, and the American people supported the Bush administration's policies, which suspended all official bilateral exchanges with Beijing and cooperated in international economic sanctions. By the early 1990s, China was still labeled as an authoritarian state by international human rights organizations.

Jiang Zemin became the chairman of the CCP after the Tiananmen events. As the head of the third generation of the CCP leadership, Jiang was challenged by a collapse of the world Communist system, including the demise of the Soviet Union in 1991. That December, Boris Yeltsin, President of the Russian Republic, announced that his country and 11 other former Soviet republics had formed the new Commonwealth of Independent States. Mikhail Gorbachev, president of the Soviet Union and general secretary of the Soviet Communist Party, found that he could no longer control the government and the country. On Christmas Day, 1991, Gorbachev resigned and recognized the new Commonwealth of Independent States. While most Communist governments went into bankruptcy and lost their power after this monumental geopolitical shift, Jiang managed a "soft landing" for the CCP, which had 60 million members.

In the early 1990s, Jiang gradually shifted the party's ideology and political goals from radical communism to moderate nationalism. The leaders began to emphasize national interests, traditions, and patriotism in order to mobilize popular support for their reform efforts. The Communist Party was able to reinvent itself without suffering unbearable financial losses. The CCP's political reorientation and propaganda demanded many changes in policy making in order to fit into the nationalist ideas and popular movements that had swept the country.

Chinese nationalism, which was deeply rooted in the hearts of several generations, has risen significantly since the 1990s as a result of explosive growth during the previous 20 years. Due to the party's extreme makeover, the Jiang administration successfully guided the state with an agenda of improving China's national defense, homeland security, sovereignty, and international status. The party's transformation, however, did not improve the relationship between individual citizens and the Chinese government. Jiang took tougher positions on Tibet, human rights issues, and Taiwan, even ordering Chinese forces to fire missiles near the island in 1996, creating another serious international crisis with the United States. The party elite has employed nationalism as an ideology to unite China, resulting in one more source of legitimacy for the CCP as the country's ruling party.

China today has little in common with the Cold War China of 1949–1978. The nation bears only the name of communism, while the government promotes business interests and the party now includes entrepreneurs, professionals, and millionaires. Official scholars have brought back Confucianism and nationalism—subjects that had been destroyed during the CCP's revolutions in the 1960s—as ruling philosophies and ideologies.

Nevertheless, this pragmatic nationalism has not yet improved the condition of civil and human rights in the PRC. The ideology is dictated by the government to pursue China's unity, strength, prosperity, and dignity rather than to value human rights and democracy at its core. This kind of nationalism emphasizes a common will and goal rather than holding human rights as its fundamental value and democracy as its desired result. Oftentimes the government has even called on individuals to scarify personal rights for the national interest.

In the summer of 2008, after the torch relay for the Olympic Games began, the world heard more and more about Chinese nationalism, especially in connection with pro-Tibet and human rights demonstrations in Europe and the United States. Many Chinese at home and even overseas regarded these protests as an attack on their basic national sovereignty and the country's identity.

CHINESE CHARACTERISTICS AND INTERNATIONAL STANDARDS

The last problem in studying China's civil rights is the gap between Chinese measures and international standards of civil liberties and human rights. China believes that it has been a victim of the international system in the past, from the Western imperialist expansion in the nineteenth century to the U.S.–Soviet Cold War in the twentieth century. This victim mentality or cultural grievance has convinced the Chinese government that it needs to find its own way rather than following others.

Many thought that a new worldview, in which China was integrated into international society, would take place after the normalization of Sino-American relations. This relationship improved when Jiang Zemin traveled to Washington, D.C., in 1997 and President Bill Clinton visited China in 1998. The Clinton administration carried out a new policy of constructive engagement with China, which it considered a "strategic partner." To engage China in the world economy, the U.S. government supported China's request to join the World Trade Organization (WTO) in the 1990s and the U.S. Congress passed the U.S.–China Trade Relations Act in 2000. The administration also backed Beijing in its bid to host the 2008 Summer Olympic Games, which, when awarded, resulted in unexpected nationwide excitement and celebration. Since joining the WTO in 2001, China has participated in many other international organizations and integrated into global trade, investment, and financial markets.

While the Chinese have become more cooperative in business and diplomacy, they have also begun to participate in international human rights organizations. The country has been increasingly active in the United Nations' Human Rights Commission, the Human Rights Council, and other international nongovernmental organizations. On October 27, 1997, China signed the International Covenant on Economic, Social, and Cultural Rights, and on February 28, 2001, this agreement was ratified at the twentieth meeting of the Ninth Chinese People's Congress Standing Committee. This marked the beginning of the Chinese government's cooperation and consideration of promoting human rights. On October 5, 1998, China had also signed the International Covenant on Civil and Political Rights.

In March 2000, Beijing hosted the Eighth Symposium on Human Rights in the Asian-Pacific Region, which was cosponsored by the UN Office of the High Commissioner for Human Rights (OHCHR). China's vice premier, Qian Qishen, attended and spoke at the event. In September, the Chinese government signed both the "Optional Protocol to the Convention on the Rights of the Child on the Sale of Children" and "Child Prostitution and Child Pornography."

U.S. president Bill Clinton and Chinese president Jiang Zemin meet before a private dinner at the Zhongnanhai leaders' compound in Beijing in 1998. (AP Photo/Greg Baker.)

In November, Mary Robinson, the UN High Commissioner for Human Rights, returned to China on invitation. She met with Jiang and Qian while she was in Beijing. She and the Chinese Foreign Ministry signed the "Memorandum of Understanding between the Ministry of Foreign Affairs of the PRC and the UN Office of the High Commissioner for Human Rights on the Mutual Agreement to Cooperate in the Development and Implementation of Technical Cooperation Programs." China agreed to cooperate with the OHCHR over the next two years to improve the country's judicial administration, human rights education, and legal system. China would also carry out cooperative projects with the OHCHR to fulfill the right to development and other rights of economy, society, and culture.

The Chinese government submitted reports to the United Nations discussing the implementation of the International Convention on the Elimination of All Forms of Racial Discrimination. It also presented to the UN its report on the implementation of the International Covenant on Economic, Social, and Cultural Rights and the International Covenant on Civil and Political Rights in the Hong Kong Special Administrative Region.

In addition to the United Nations, China communicated with individual countries to discuss the human rights issue, as well. In 1997, China and Great Britain established the "UK–China Human Rights Dialogue." China held its ninth and tenth dialogues with the European Union during February and September 2000, and the two powers also held their fourth and fifth judicial symposiums in May and December of the same year. China and Britain held the fourth and fifth dialogues on human rights. In August, China held its fourth human rights dialogue with Australia. And also in that year, China, Canada, and Norway held the Third Symposium on Human Rights in Bangkok, Thailand; at the symposium, the participating countries passed the Bangkok Declaration.

China's policy of engagement reflects a conscious decision to take a more active role in establishing systems of normative global practices. The country intends to be seen as a team player, and there was a hope that the nation's participation and acceptance of international law would improve its domestic human rights and civil liberties.

As a new member of the global community, however, the PRC has not always followed all international standards, but has instead adapted the regulations selectively. While Hu Jintao, head of the CCP's fourth generation of leadership, was cooperative on certain issues, his government did not always go with the West, especially the United States. President George W. Bush, trying to include China in the war against terror after September 11, 2001, and to coordinate responses to the crises with North Korea, asked China to be a "responsible stakeholder" in multilateral national efforts. But Beijing considers many matters, including the human rights and civil liberties, to be domestic problems and believes that no foreign government or organization should interfere in its internal affairs. The West believes in natural rights that cannot be taken from people nor given away, but the Chinese government looks at these same "rights" as privileges that are granted and can be withheld by the state.

China's implementation of international laws and agreements in the area of trade, such as the WTO, depends largely on its understanding of the accords and on national governmental capabilities in local communities. The country continues to face criticism over its willingness and ability to meet its international obligations, especially in applying global standards in such areas as labor, health, gender, and especially human rights. As previously discussed, the Chinese government's statements on human rights are often different from international norms, particularly in their focus on hierarchies of rights and local conditions of development. Its reliance on the right to participate in the development of global legal standards has been used to justify its selective adoption and frequent rejections of international norms. The country has its own normative principles, which have been described as the "Chinese characteristics."

This term, "Chinese characteristics," is used as a descriptor for the methods and rules particular to the PRC that are used in the practice of business or law. These constrain human rights and civil liberties by limiting their protections to those who are willing and able to protect the interests of the state and support the party's rule. The Chinese characteristics also put limitations on the international community by demanding that other countries respect China's sovereignty, the limits it has placed on specific regions and populations, and the preservation of its governance priorities as preconditions for the nation's compliance with international human rights standards. These factors suggest that, during its reforms, China requested the international legal community to accept the state's judicial and political systems as exceptional cases. The PRC's citation of the Chinese characteristics to support the primacy of government control of human rights enforcement cannot, however, replace the necessity of conforming to international standards in the nation's quest to achieve global legitimacy.

Freedom of religion is a valuable example. The Chinese government insists that each country has its own history, culture, and national conditions that determine the extent to which the country protects religious expression. Therefore, the PRC protects the freedom not to believe, ensuring freedom of religion completely. According to Beijing, religion is a person's personal choice, whereas creating a powerful and prosperous democratic socialist country with advanced culture and the ability to maintain national dignity and sovereignty should be the common goal and in the basic interest of all Chinese, regardless of ethnic group or religious persuasion. Since the 1980s, the Chinese government has accused some churches, temples, and religious groups of engaging in illegal and criminal activities under the guise of religion.

Some of their leaders and members have been jailed or even executed because these "pseudo-religious doctrines" were said to have distorted social order, created heresies, deceived the masses, refused to obey state law and decrees, and incited rebellion.

The Chinese government is most concerned with Tibetan Buddhists and has been targeting their religious-based separatist movement, which receives various forms of support from abroad. The U.S. and other Western governments, as well as the UN's OHCHR, continue to urge China to guarantee civil liberties and punish officers of the state who violate these rights. Nongovernmental organizations such as Human Rights Watch, Amnesty International, the Committee to Protect Journalists, and Reporters without Borders have also joined the effort to persuade Beijing to allow citizens to express both grievances and constructive criticism, to work more actively and constructively with Buddhist and other religious groups, and to prevent officials from interfering in this process or exacting revenge on those who participate.

Although Chinese leaders have promised to improve civil liberties and human rights, problems and developmental challenges continue to increase. The country's dramatic economic expansion has convinced the government that they have a workable and manageable system that allows not merely institutional survival but success. It may take another generation of leadership to make the necessary substantial changes in the Chinese government and society, and one must continuously reevaluate its policy decisions and make concerted and persistent efforts to understand the factors that shape them.

This book covers the development of principal existing civil rights and liberties in China. It situates the legal system and landmark cases in the context of Chinese society while taking into account their patterns, progress, and challenges. This volume divides civil liberties into several phases. Chapter 1 provides an overview of civil rights by examining the country's constitutional history from the founding of the PRC in 1949 to the present. Chapter 2 covers freedom of speech and freedom of assembly since 2000, focusing on the political expression of individuals and the mass media, regulations on organization and associations, and problems with law enforcement and political dissent. Chapter 3 discusses freedom of religion by tracing its expression, governmental interference, and religious life in today's China. Chapter 4 examines public information and government regulations, individual expression, the media, and social networks such as radio, television, and the Internet. Chapter 5 details Chinese citizens' right to privacy, such as the extent to which the government does or does not refrain from regulating one's personal life, particularly in the cases of contraception, abortion, the one-child policy, and ending one's life. Chapter 6 focuses on the rights of the criminally accused by examining governmental interference in one's legal rights, such as freedom from unreasonable searches, unfair interrogation, self-incrimination, or cruel and unusual punishment. It is also devoted to due process for the accused and legal protection of their rights, including those of having a lawyer in a criminal proceeding, a fair trial, and appellate review.

Understanding China's legal system and the challenges it faces is one of the most important tasks of the twenty-first century. Even though it has the world's highest economic growth rate, China is not yet a country ruled by law. The country must face its own problems consisting of, but not limited to, interference in personal life, human rights violations, prisoner labor and abuse, court corruption, and inconsistency in legal practice. These factors all slow down its democratization and impede the improvement of the Sino-U.S. relationship. The U.S. government must work with China on developing shared political, social, and judicial objectives and thereby draw the PRC further into the international system. China, in turn, must live up to its international obligations and global standards of civil and human rights.

Chronology

1949 **September 29:** The Chinese People's Political Consultative Conference (CPPCC) passes the Common Program as China's provisional constitution.

October 1: Mao Zedong proclaims the founding of the People's Republic of China (PRC) in Beijing. Mao becomes the chairman of the Central Military Commission of the Central Government. The First CPPCC Plenary Session creates the Supreme Court with Shen Junru as president.

1950 The Marriage Law, Trade Union Law, and Agrarian Reform Law are promulgated.

September: China launches a mass movement to suppress counterrevolutionaries in rural areas, with 1.27 million incarcerated and 800,000 executed.

October 19: The PRC sends a large number of Chinese troops to the Korean War as a "volunteer force" to fight against the UN forces.

1951 The government launches the Three Antis and Five Antis movements in the cities to support its "War to Resist America and Aid Korea." The Central Government signs an agreement with the Tibetan government on "Measures for the Liberation of Tibet," reorganizing Tibet as part of China and granting the region autonomous status.

July 10: Truce negotiations begin in Korea.

1952   Mao calls for a national movement to learn from the Soviet Union under the leadership of Joseph Stalin. The Three Antis and Five Antis campaigns continue against manufacturing, finance, and trading operations in private sector and are viewed as the precursor to a looming de-privatization movement. China continues fighting the Korean War while negotiating for peace.

1953   The first Five-Year Plan (1953–1957) starts.
          January: A committee, headed by Mao, is created by the twenty-first meeting of the Central Government to draft a constitution.
          February 11: At its twenty-second meeting, the government passes the Electoral Law, which is published on March 1.
          July 27: The armistice ending the Korean War is signed.

1954   **September 20:** The First National People's Congress (NPC) passes the constitution and elects Mao as the PRC's president, Zhu De as vice president, Zhou Enlai as premier, Liu Shaoqi as chairman of the NPC, and Dong Biwu as president of the Supreme Court. The First NPC Plenary Session then creates the Ministry of Justice and promulgates the Court Organization Law and Procuratorial Law.
          December: The NPC issues regulations on arrest, detention, and public security organizations.

1955   **June 1:** The Ministry of Internal Affairs publishes the Marriage Registration Law.
          July 1: The State Council issues instructions to establish the Residential Registration System.
          July: The Ministry of Public Security issues regulations on transportation, traffic, radio, telegrams, and electronic communication.
          July 30: The Second NPC Plenary issues the Military Service Law.

1956   **May 8:** The NPC and CPPCC hold a joint conference and decide important legal issues, including no public trials and depriving criminals of political right for life.
          September 15–27: The Eighth CCP National Congress convenes and reelects Mao as chairman for its six million

party members. Mao calls for the "Blooming of the Hundred Flowers" movement.

October 10: The State Council issues regulations on the police and law enforcement ranking system.

1957   Mao launches the Anti-Rightist movement.

August 3: The NPC establishes the Reeducation Through Labor (RTL) system to detain "counterrevolutionaries" without trial for a period of between one and twelve years, working as menial labor on state-owned farms or in factories.

October 22: The NPC issues regulations on public security, management, and punishments.

1958   The second Five-Year Plan (1958–1962) begins.

May 5–23: The Second Plenum of the Eighth CCP Central Committee passes a new general line with the phrase "more, faster, better, and more economically soundly" to build socialist economy. As part of the general line, the Great Leap Forward movement begins.

November 28–December 10: The Sixth Plenum decides to launch the People's Commune movement as part of the general line.

1959   **March:** The State Council appoints the Panchen Lama to chair the Tibetan Preparatory Committee. People's Liberation Army (PLA) troops suppress the Tibetan rebellion. The Dalai Lama flees to India.

April: The Second NPC elects Liu Shaoqi as the PRC's president and Xie Juezai as Supreme Court president. The Ministry of Justice is closed until 1979.

July 2–August 16: The CCP Eighth Plenum accuses Peng Dehuai and some generals of forming a "right opportunist clique" in the party and army.

September 17: Lin Biao replaces Peng as defense minister.

1960   The great Sino-Soviet polemic debate begins and lasts for three years. Mao criticizes Soviet leader Nikita Khrushchev as a "revisionist" who has betrayed Communists throughout the world.

August 13: By this date, the Soviet Union calls for all 12,000 Russian experts to leave China and terminates all Soviet economic and military aid.

1961   China experiences a serious economic depression known as the Three Hard Years caused by "natural disasters." By this year, serious shortages of food, fuel, and other daily needs claim more than 30 million lives. The CCP calls for new efforts to overcome the economic difficulties by party members, who total 17.3 million by June.

1962   **September 24–27:** The CCP holds its Tenth Plenum of the Eighth Central Committee and emphasizes the class struggle.
October 20: The Sino-Indian War breaks out along the Tibetan border.
November 22: The Chinese government announces a cease-fire along the Chinese-Indian border and begins to pull Chinese troops out of Indian territories.

1963   **April 12–May 16:** President Liu visits Indonesia, Burma, Vietnam, and Cambodia.
May: Mao starts the socialist education movement, also known as the Four Cleanups, in rural areas.
December: Premier Zhou begins travels that will take him to 14 countries in Africa by the end of January.

1964   **October 16:** China carries out its first nuclear bomb test.
December 20: The Third NPC opens, running through January 4. Liu is reelected as president and Zhou as premier. Zhou calls for the Four Modernizations.

1965   **May 14:** China conducts its second nuclear test.
July: China begins to send troops to Vietnam, including PLA surface-to-air missile, antiaircraft artillery, combat engineering, and logistics units.
September: The Tibet Autonomous Region is formally inaugurated.

1966   **May:** Mao launches the Great Proletarian Cultural Revolution, a nationwide political struggle accompanied by extensive purges. The students organize the Red Guards as the driving force for the movement. All schools and colleges are closed. The masses are urged to be guided by Mao's Thought instead of law.

October: President Liu, Vice Premier Deng Xiaoping, and many other high-ranking government officials are publicly criticized and purged; some are tortured and killed by the Red Guards.

1967 **January:** The mass organizations begin to overtake the power of the authorities in Shanghai; other cities follow. The legal system is attacked as many existing government mechanisms are totally paralyzed. Armed clashes take place between different mass organizations when all of them try to take over the local government.

July: An armed clash occurs in Hubei, and more than 180,000 civilians and soldiers are killed or wounded. To prevent civil war, 2.8 million officers and soldiers of the PLA are employed to restore order through military administrative committees.

1968 **October 13–31:** The Twelfth Plenum of the CCP Eighth Central Committee is held and officially purges President Liu and many leaders from the party, government, and PLA. By the end of the year, China has sent 23 divisions, totaling 320,000 troops, to Vietnam.

1969 **March:** Sino-Soviet border conflicts begin at Zhenbao (Damansky) Island, Heilongjiang, and then continue in many places along the border in the Xinjiang Uyghur Autonomous Region.

April 1–24: The CCP holds the Ninth National Congress and recognizes Lin as Mao's successor.

April 28: The First Plenum of the CCP Ninth Central Committee reelects Mao as party chairman and elects Lin as the vice chairman.

November 12: President Liu dies after two years of detention.

1970 Sino-Soviet border conflicts continue.

April: China launches its first satellite. Henry Kissinger and Le Duc Tho begin secret talks to end the Vietnam War. China withdraws its troops from Vietnam.

1971 **September 13:** Lin and his family are killed in a plane crash in Mongolia. Mao begins another top-down purge and shakeup in the military and appoints Ye Jianying as defense minister.

October: China is admitted to the United Nations.

1972   **February:** President Richard Nixon visits China, where he signs the joint Shanghai Communiqué agreeing that there is but one China and that Taiwan is a part of China.

1973   **August 24–28:** The CCP Tenth National Congress is held and again reelects Mao as the chairman. The United States and China announce their intention to establish liaison offices in each other's capital.

1974   **October:** Mao suggests bringing Deng Xiaoping back from the purge as first vice premier. After his return, Deng also serves as the vice chairman of the CCP Central Military Commission and chief of staff of the PLA.

1975   **January 13:** The Fourth NPC promulgates the second constitution, which minimizes or completely eliminates the courts and procurates and does not retain individual rights such as that of freedom of speech and press.

         December: President Gerald Ford visits Beijing and agrees to terminate the U.S.–Taiwan mutual security treaty and withdraw U.S. military forces from the island.

1976   **January 8:** Zhou Enlai dies.

         July 28: An earthquake measuring 7.8 on the Richter scale rocks Tangshan and becomes the most deadly earthquake of the twentieth century with about 240,000–255,000 people killed, 164,000 severely injured, and 779,000 others injured.

         September 9: Mao Zedong dies at age 82. Mao's death ends the Cultural Revolution, in which an estimated 100 million people were killed, injured, or otherwise persecuted or victimized.

         October: Maoist leaders called the "Gang of Four," led by Mao's widow, Jiang Qing, are arrested by Hua Guofeng.

         November: The Criminal Code is issued with 22 crimes, including rape and robbery, punishable by the death penalty.

1977   Official statistics show that more than 250 million people are below the poverty line.

July 16–21: The Third Plenum of the CCP Tenth Central Committee supports Hua's leadership and the purge of the Gang of Four.

August 12–18: The CCP Eleventh National Congress meets and elects Hua as chairman with Ye, Deng, Li Xiannian, and Wang Dongxing as vice chairmen.

1978   Deng Xiaoping becomes the key leader and begins an unprecedented reform program and opening up to the world to modernize China after his historical speech, "Emancipate the Mind," at the Third Plenum of the Eleventh CCP Central Committee, on December 13.

March 5: The Fifth NPC promulgates the third constitution. The new constitution restores the courts and procurates and reinstates some of the citizens' rights.

Fall: A new democracy movement, the "Democracy Walls," begins to take hold in several major cities.

1979   **January 1:** China establishes diplomatic relations with the United States. Deng becomes the first PRC leader to visit America, holding talks with President Jimmy Carter and signing the protocols.

February 17: China invades Vietnam with 200,000 PLA troops. The struggles to save the Democracy Walls become the "Beijing Spring" movement, which is suppressed by the government.

July: The Fifth NPC announces the Criminal Law and the Organic Law of the local governments. The Ministry of Justice reopens after 20 years. The State Council decrees supplementary regulations regarding the RTL system. The family planning and birth control policy known as "one-child policy" begins.

1980   **August 30–September 10:** The Third Plenary Session of the Fifth NPC passes the new Citizenship Law, Marriage Law, Joint Adventure Income Tax, and Individual Income Tax Law.

November 20–December 29: The Supreme Court holds open trials of the Gang of Four. The State Council issues new regulations regarding the RTL system by combining forced

labor education and detention-investigation into a single practice to allow detention without trial of up to four years for
minor offenses.

1981   The CCP Central Military Commission elects Deng as
chairman. Hu Yaobang replaces Hua Guofeng as chairman
of the CCP Central Committee. Both Hu and Zhao Ziyang
are appointed vice chairmen.

1982   **September 1–October 1:** The CCP holds its Twelfth
National Congress.
December 4: The Fifth Plenary Session of the Fifth NPC
adopts a new constitution, which remains in effect today,
incorporating some amendments during the 1990s. It recognizes the people's liberties and institutionalizes these rights
into a component of the judicial system. The constitution
and the Law on the Organization of Courts provide the
accused with the right to have a proper defense.

1983   The People's Armed Police (PAP) is established. The Ministry of Foreign Affairs starts a spokesperson system, opening
an information channel only for diplomatic and other important political occasions.

1984   **April:** President Ronald Reagan visits China and meets with
Deng.
October: The Third Plenum of the Twelfth CCP Central
Committee decides to reform the economic structure. Four-
teen coastal cities and the island of Hainan are opened to
foreign investment.

1985   President Li Xiannian visits Washington and signs a pact
allowing the sale of U.S. nonmilitary technology to China.
Vice President George H. W. Bush visits China. Deng is
named *Time* magazine's Man of the Year for the second time.

1986   Chinese courts handle two million cases this year. Authorities send 870,000 persons to the RTL system—detention
without trial from one to four years in the forced labor
camps—each year in the 1980s.

1987   China has only four law schools and 25 law departments in
universities, and just 26,000 lawyers across the country, while

the government carries out at least 200 death sentences every month. The accused are often denied a meaningful appeal and executed on the day of their conviction.

1988 **April:** The First Session of the Seventh NPC adopts two constitutional amendments on private property and protection of the ownership of the private property. The constitution recognizes "private economy" as a "supplement to the socialist state economy." China ratifies the UN Convention against Torture and signs the International Covenant on Civil and Political Rights.

1989 **May:** Hundreds of thousands of students and citizens hold demonstrations in Beijing, which later spread to 116 cities. **May 6–16:** Students encamp at Tiananmen Square and begin a hunger strike.
May 19: The government declares martial law and deploys 22 infantry divisions in the cities.
June 3–4: PLA troops open fire at the students and citizens at Tiananmen Square, with an estimated 1,000 casualties. **October:** The government issues the Act on Marches and Demonstration, limiting citizens' rights to assemble and demonstrate. The State Council issues the Registration of Social Organizations, including many restrictions on the freedom of association.

1990 **April:** President Yang Shangkun promulgates the Basic Law of the Hong Kong Special Administrative Region adopted by the Seventh NPC, scheduled to take effect on July 1, 1997.

1991 The State Council issues the Provisions on the Administration of Religious Activities within the Territory of the PRC. In the wake of the 1989 Tiananmen Square incident, Jiang Zemin becomes the top leader as the chairman of both the party Central Committee and Central Military Commission.

1992 The State Bureau of Religions of the State Council approves the succession of the Living Buddha of the Seventeenth Karmapa.
May: Falun Gong, one of the *qigong*-based exercise groups, is established.

1993   **March:** The First Session of the Eighth NPC makes nine important changes as amendments to the constitution, including some changes in the preamble. It allows the household production responsibility system to replace the people's communes and the private management of state enterprises.

1994   The number of lawyers increases to 70,000, but the country has 3.85 million legal cases this year; the courts report hearing 3.6 million cases. As a result, many defendants do not have legal aid or a chance for appeal.
            January: The State Council promulgates the Regulations on the Administration of Sites for Religious Activities, placing severe restrictions on family churches and citizens' faith-based activities.

1995   Only 6 percent of Chinese judges have college degrees (not necessarily a law degree). The new criminal code increases the number of crimes punishable by the death penalty from 26 to 60.

1996   The State Council issues the State Administration for Religious Affairs.
            Spring: China fires missiles near Taiwan and conducts a military exercise in the Taiwan Strait.
            May: The NPC passes new legislation to reform criminal justice procedures and the legal profession. For the first time, China recognizes that lawyers represent their clients, not the state, according to the Lawyer's Law.

1997   An amendment of the criminal code adds eight more crimes that are punishable by the death penalty. The Standing Committee of the NPC amends the Criminal Law.
            February 19: Deng Xiaoping dies at the age of 93. **March 14:** The Law on National Defense is adopted, defining the mission of the PAP.
            July 1: Britain hands Hong Kong back to China.
            September: Jiang Zemin meets President Bill Clinton in Washington.
            October 27: China signs the International Covenant on Economic, Social, and Cultural Rights.

1998   Clinton meets Jiang in Beijing to challenge China on human rights issues. Statistics show that more than 42 million people are below the poverty line. The government conducts an internal shakeup of the judiciary, resulting in the punishment of more than 4,200 judicial branch employees. The country accounts for over 70 percent of criminals executed in the world per year.
October 5: China signs the International Covenant on Civil and Political Rights.

1999   The courts handle six million cases this year.
March: The Second Session of the Ninth NPC adopts six constitutional amendments for enforcement. The constitution for the first time redefines the socialist state economy as a socialist market economy. The Supreme Court issues its first five-year plan for legal reforms.
July: The authorities outlaw the Falun Gong movement and arrest 90,000 members. **December:** Portugal returns Macao to China.

2000   The CCP Central Committee and the State Council issue a joint decision to enforce the one-child policy. Official records show 3,082 fatalities in coal mining. About 20 percent of Chinese judges have college degrees. The courts report hearing 5.85 million cases this year, including 560,000 criminal, 4.37 million civil, and 87,000 administrative cases. Police arrest 635,000 of 720,000 suspects and file charges against 610,000 detainees. An estimated 2,000 Falun Gong practitioners die as a result of official persecution. The PAP comprises one million members.

2001   The Law on Population and Birth Planning is promulgated to provide a general framework and more details for provincial regulations and operations.
May: Hundreds of residents of Shangzhou, Shaanxi, are found to be infected with AIDS, a rate of 4 percent. As many as 100 million rural laborers are on the move and seeking work in cities.
October: President George W. Bush visits Shanghai. China joins the WTO.

2002   The State Council revises the Regulations on Prohibiting the Use of Child Labor. Official records show an annual fatality count in coal mining of 3,790. The government promulgates provisions on administrative cases to tighten law enforcement procedures. The courts report hearing 5.58 million cases this year.

February: President Bush visits Beijing.

November: Severe Acute Respiratory Syndrome (SARS) breaks out in southern China.

2003   China has 31 provincial bureaus of public security, 356 metropolitan police departments, 2,972 county police headquarters, and 41,941 local police stations. The PAP has 31 armies, including 508 armed police regiments and 42 special regiments, including helicopter, artillery, chemical, and tank regiments. The PAP also has 32 commanding officer academies and 29 hospitals. Chinese police crack 2.3 million criminal cases. The courts investigate 635,000 criminal first-instance cases and 88,000 administrative lawsuits this year. Procuratorial organs appeal against court judgments of 2,906 criminal cases that they deem incorrectly tried. There are 58,000 mass protests this year.

July 31: There are 5,328 SARS cases and 349 fatalities. Official records show 4,143 fatalities in coal mining.

September: The State Council revises the Publications Administration Regulations and Regulations Governing the Administration of Audio-Visual Products.

November: The Supreme Court formulates 20 documents of judicial interpretation of criminal, civil, and administrative law enforcement and regulations on legal aid. The Ministry of Justice formulates and implements the Regulations on Reform through Education in Prisons, Law on Prisons, and Regulations on the Procedures for Applications by Prisons for Commutation and Parole.

2004   By this year, the State Council has issued 800 administrative laws and regulations accounted for more than 60 percent of all of those in China. There are 74,000 mass protests this year. The courts report hearing 5.54 million cases.

March: The Second Session of the Tenth NPC adopts and publishes 14 important amendments to the constitution. Among the most important of these is the phrase added to Article 33: "The state respects and guarantees human rights." This marks the first time the constitution has contained mention of human rights. Other laws are also adopted, including the Law on National Regional Autonomy, General Principles of the Civil Law, Education Law, and Labor Law.

April: The State Council revises the Law on the Protection of Women's Rights and Interests.

September: A researcher for the *New York Times* is detained by authorities.

November: The government launches a new detention campaign targeting writers, journalists, and political commentators.

2005   Mass protests increase to 87,000 for the year. Authorities have 32 journalists in jail this year. For the first time, about 50 percent of Chinese judges have college degrees.

March: The Third Session of the Tenth NPC adopts new laws, including the Compulsory Education Law, Electoral Law of the People's Congress, Organic Law of the Villagers' Committees, and Advertisement Law. It amends the Law on the Protection of Women's Rights and Interests by including a ban on sexual harassment, human trafficking, and sex trade, which remain significant problems.

June: The Ministry of Public Security estimates that 10,000 women and children are abducted and sold each year, and two to four million women are involved in prostitution.

August: The government spends at least $800 million on an elaborate system of censorship, called the "Great Firewall of China," to control its citizens online.

December: Official records show 6,000 miners died this year. China signs two key international human rights treaties that include articles against the death penalty. Even though the execution total declines, the country still tops the world in execution with a total of 3,400 this year.

2006   More than 80,000 incidents of social unrest and protest take place this year. China now has 490,000 police, 150,000

detectives and investigators, and 1.5 million members of the PAP. At least 930 cases of police torture take place. More than 300 police officers have been killed every year since 1993.
November: Official statistics show that more than 31 million people are below the poverty line. About 30 percent of families suffer from domestic violence, while 90 percent of the victims are women and children.
December: The courts report having heard 5.7 million cases and tried 933,156 criminal cases during the year. Only 30 percent of the defendants have a lawyer or legal consultant on their case. The conviction rate for first- and second-instance criminal trials is more than 99.85 percent; only about 1,400 out of nearly a million criminal cases result in a verdict of not guilty.

2007 China has more than 580,000 police, 150,000 detectives, and 250,000 traffic cops and special police, all of whom are under the control of the Ministry of Public Security. Authorities arrest 270 priests of underground Christian churches this year. Official records show that 101,510 administrative lawsuits are filed against the government this year. The country has more than 150,000 licensed lawyers. A total of 1.8 million prisoners, including 29 journalists, are in jail.
January 1: The government issues temporary regulations (through October 17, 2008) to give foreign correspondents the freedom to interview anyone who consents and to express their own opinions before and during the Olympic Games. After the Chinese Catholic bishop Fu Tieshan dies, the government appoints his successor, usurping the authority of the pope.
June: Xinjiang authorities began to collect Muslims' passports in order to prevent them from making non-state-approved pilgrimages to Mecca. The NPC passes the Law of Laborer Contracts.
August: The CCP Central Committee establishes the Bureau of Internet Propaganda, and the State Council establishes the Bureau of Internet to censor online activities. They issue the Regulations for the Management of Internet Publishing and bring online magazines under the same controls as print publications.

September: The Ministry of the Information Industry issues a new set of rules aimed at curbing the spread of interactive Internet sites. Authorities close 14,000 "illegal" websites.

October: British TV reporters are arrested during their interview and filming, just one of 160 reported incidents of harassment of foreign journalists conducting interviews this year.

2008   151,000 party and government officials are disciplined during the year. The Foreign Correspondents' Club of China reports 178 incidents of harassment by Chinese authorities of foreign journalists when they were conducting interviews this year.

March 14: Buddhist riots—the "3/14 Riots"—occur in Lhasa. Authorities arrested Tibetans arbitrarily, including monks and nuns. Official state media report the detention of 4,434 persons.

March 28: The government confirms 28 civilians and one police officer died and 325 civilians were injured during the 3/14 Riots; the India-based Tibetan government-in-exile puts the figures at more than 220 Tibetans killed and 7,000 arrested.

April 29: The Lhasa Intermediate Court sentences 30 Tibetans to three years to life in prison for their participations in the 3/14 Riots.

May 12: An earthquake measuring 8.0 on the Richter scale hits Wenchuan County, Sichuan. Official statistics show at least 69,000 people killed, 374,000 injured, 18,000 missing, and 4.8 million homeless.

August: The Propaganda Department of the CCP Central Committee issues a 21-point directive outlining how the domestic media should handle certain stories during the Olympics.

August 8–24: China hosts the Olympic Games in Beijing, with the participation of 10,500 athletes in 302 events of 28 sports.

September: In Xinjiang, police detain and beat two Japanese journalists attempting to cover the aftermath of a deadly attack on a PAP unit.

October 17: The government makes permanent rules granting foreign journalists greater freedoms by eliminating previous requirements for them to seek permission from local

officials before conducting interviews in a province or locality.
October: The NPC makes 15 laws and law-related decisions concerning national defense and the armed forces.

2009   The government sentences and executes four Tibetans in connection with their involvement with the 3/14 Riots.

July 5: Tens of thousands of Uyghur demonstrators gather in the city center of Urumqi, Xinjiang, protesting the government's handling of the death of two Uyghur workers. After confrontations with police, the demonstration escalates into riots, with 197 people dead and 1,721 others injured, according to the government reports.

July 18: The World Uyghur Congress reports 600 dead during the "7/5 Riots" in Xinjiang. Officials confirm more than 1,500 rioters have been arrested. The government cuts off almost all Internet access to the 19 million people in Xinjiang.

November 14–17: President Barack Obama visits China and explains the significance of civil liberties to Chinese students in Shanghai.

December 29: British citizen Akmal Shaikh is executed by lethal injection by Chinese authorities after being convicted of drug smuggling in October.

December: Authorities sentence 22 Uyghurs to death for their participation in the 7/5 Riots.

2010   China calls for a campaign against "illegal text messages" and "unhealthy content." Cellular phone service companies are required to automatically scan text messages for keywords provided by the police and to forward offending messages to the police for evaluation.

January: Google announces that the company will no longer cooperate with China's censorship laws.

February 12: The government lifts its online blackout of Xinjiang, which has been enforced since July 2009, just before the Chinese Lunar New Year.

February 18: President Obama meets the Dalai Lama at the White House.

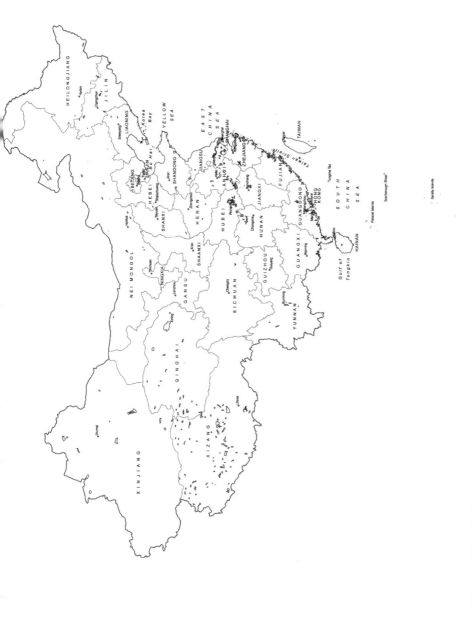

Map of China. (Digital Wisdom.)

Chapter 1

A Constitutional History

Since the founding of the People's Republic of China (PRC), China has promulgated four state constitutions, in 1954, 1975, 1978, and 1982. The current constitution was adopted by the Fifth National People's Congress on December 4, 1982. Since then, the constitution has had some important changes and revisions in 1988, 1993, 1999, and 2004. Even though some civil liberties and legal codes were provided by the constitution, many of them have not been enacted until recent years. The Chinese constitution has gone through several periods of acceptance, rejection, and rewriting in the past 60 years.

After the first constitution was promulgated in 1954, it encountered challenges from some radical political movements and social experiments during the 1960s and met with doubt during the 1970s. However, since the 1980s, the constitution has been improved to accommodate China's new era of development. The current constitution, with its amendments that have been incorporated through 2004, has finally recognized the people's liberties and institutionalized these rights into a component of the nation's judicial system that had been created with the founding of the PRC in 1949.

In preparation for the emergence of the new Communist state in September 1949, the Chinese Communist Party (CCP) leadership named the new country the People's Republic of China in order to differentiate it from the old Nationalist state, the Republic of China, established in 1911. The "people's republic," however, did not empower the people or protect their civil rights and liberties. During its early years, the new China instead followed the Soviet authoritarian

A customer reaches for an amended copy of *China's Communist Party Constitution* in a bookstore in Beijing. The constitution includes the "Three Represents", Chinese president Jiang Zemin's personal theory for the role of the Communist Party, which was enshrined in the party charter at the 16th Communist Party Congress. The book, of which 850,000 copies are being printed in its first issue, sells for 2.3 Yuan (US 27 cents) each. (AP Photo/Greg Baker.)

model and limited the people's rights by breaking with tradition and expanding state power through political campaigns and class struggle. After the Sino-Soviet split in the 1960s, the Chinese government failed to improve the condition of civil liberties and provide for the protection of individuals. Between 1949 and 1990, Chinese society was centered around a unitary party-state that maintained complete control of all social resources. The CCP's center used the government—including the courts, law enforcement, and the legal system—to serve its Communist political agenda as a totalitarian authority. The constitution of the three decades preceding 1982 was merely a history of the party's experiment in political establishment and institutional dictatorship, which created many obstacles to serious legal reform at the end of the century.

FORMATIVE YEARS, 1949–1954

On September 29, 1949, the First Chinese People's Political Consultative Conference (CPPCC) passed the Common Program at its First Plenary Session in Beijing. The Common Program served as China's provisional constitution from 1949 to 1954 and stipulated the freedoms and liberties of the Chinese people. It established the Central People's Government (CPG) under the leadership of the Chinese Communist Party, with Mao Zedong, the CCP chairman, as the first PRC president. The First Plenary Session of the CPPCC created the Supreme People's Court and appointed Shen Junru as the first president of that body. Nevertheless, the CCP leadership followed the Soviet model and established Communist control over the country through violent class struggle. The Common Program was not strictly enforced by the CCP-controlled government, but was rather used for propaganda purposes. The party center had its own political agenda that limited people's rights in the new China.

"Democratic Dictatorship"

The new government announced that freedoms and rights were not for all of China's citizens. In October 1949, President Mao proclaimed that his government was a democratic coalition under the CCP leadership, a "people's democratic dictatorship" (sometimes called a "proletarian democratic dictatorship"), to unify possible support for the regime against enemies.[1] Using Marxist-Leninist theories, the CCP emphasized the class-based nature of the society and legal system. In the old capitalist state, the law had favored the rich and wealthy, while under socialism, the party believed it should protect the poor or proletarians against the former ruling classes, who were now enemies of the state. The Communist government, drawing a line between enemies and allies, identified supporters of the new regime and sought to destroy the old social order by targeting the wealthy gentry, landlords, and social elites, who, as leaders of "old China," could potentially lead resistance against the new state.

To solidify this new establishment, the CPG implemented discrimination against millions of people on the basis of their wealth or "class origin." Those regarded as having a "bad class origin" were considered possible threats to the new China. They and their children, and even

A Chinese propaganda poster from 1952 titled *The Glory of Mao's Ideologies Brightens up the New China*. The poster depicts Chinese leader Mao Zedong standing in front of a red flag on which appear portraits of prominent Communists Joseph Stalin, Vladimir Lenin, Friedrich Engels, and Karl Marx. (Courtesy of the Library of Congress.)

their grandchildren, were treated as social and political outcasts, discriminated against in education, employment, and daily life, and often viewed as potential criminals who were watched with suspicion. Mao justified the necessity of class struggle and stated that the Chinese people could never have any rights or liberties until they took them away from their social enemies, the "counterrevolutionaries." Thus, under the people's democratic dictatorship, class struggle continued year after year through ruthless suppression, antagonistic contradiction, and massive violations of civil and human rights through the 1950s, 1960s, and 1970s.

Mass Movements

Their experience of working with the masses during the Chinese civil war had convinced the CCP leaders that they could consolidate power and solve the country's problems by thorough mobilization, such as they had achieved in the "people's war" of their armed revolution. During the 1950s, Mao launched one political movement after another to engage the masses in the class struggle and to eliminate those labeled as potential or already active counterrevolutionaries through initiatives such as land reform, the Three Antis movement, Five Antis movement, and Anti-Rightist movement. All of these campaigns turned into violent reactions against millions of Chinese people.

During the 1950s, the CCP believed it needed a charismatic authority and absolute power to achieve its idealistic goals. The leadership had learned from their successful military struggle for power against the Guomindang (GMD, the Chinese Nationalist Party) that violent means were necessary not only for establishing national power but also for continuing their Communist revolution after the founding of the PRC. The ideology, experience, and nature of this transformation left little room for the Chinese people's civil liberties.

The efforts to suppress counterrevolutionaries in 1950–1951 became a brutal struggle against the former officials and supporters of the GMD government. In late September 1950, when the campaign started, Mao asked the new government not to kill a single agent of the enemy, but simply to arrest them and place them in jail. Soon, however, the Chinese leaders changed their position and called for the execution of all enemy elements. The new regime realized the necessity of stamping out all resistance in its efforts to consolidate political control. The campaign then became swift and decisive, as thousands of suspected enemies of the revolution were rounded up, tried—sometimes on extremely limited evidence—and arbitrarily sentenced; according to Mao, around 1.27 million were incarcerated and 800,000 were executed.

The Common Program stipulated, in Article 75, "By law, the trials in the People's Court shall be conducted through the people's assessors system."[2] Many of the accused, however, did not have a lawyer, hearing, or even trial before they were sentenced or executed. Through a massive peasant movement, landlords and rich peasants as a social class were eliminated through a campaign that shocked much of the rural population, most of whom were unaware of the wrath of the revolutionary state.

While this suppression of counterrevolutionaries disturbed rural areas, two additional movements, the Three Antis and Five Antis, expressed the will of the new regime to impose order in industry and commerce by all-out assaults on the bourgeoisie in the cities. In 1950–1953, China's intervention in the Korean War dragged the country into a significant conflict with the United Nations and U.S. forces in the Korean Peninsula. To meet the drastic war needs, the CCP had to strengthen its economic and financial control more than ever. The government therefore launched the Three Antis and Five Antis movements in 1951–1954 to target the private manufacturing, commerce, trade, financial, and real estate sectors in urban areas.

The Party Center mobilized and encouraged manufacturing workers, company employees, and bank clerks to report their employers' wrongdoing and the companies' illegal activities. Most private entrepreneurs were found guilty in one way or another, and almost all of their businesses, properties, and even their homes in the cities were confiscated by the government—an action made possible by the practical nonexistence of private property and individual rights. The criteria for punishable crimes and their accompanying sentences became noticeably harsher against business owners, and more than 200,000 of these individuals and their families died during these two campaigns, resulting in the virtual elimination of the bourgeoisie as a class.

These movements made China a Soviet-style state, in which the government owned 98 percent of all industry, commerce, finance, and trade. The Chinese leaders had constructed a Communist institution that put severe limits on individual freedoms, including movement, employment, and economic activities.

Political Organizations

Aside from the successful political campaigns, the CCP also effectively established several state organizations at the grassroots level to "represent" the masses and curb the complaints about the lack of people's liberties and basic rights. These organizations, such as the Chinese Communist Youth League (CCYL), All-China Federation of Trade Unions (ACFTU), All-China Women's Association, and the Chinese Peasant Association, were and still are under the leadership of the CCP.

For example, the CCYL (also known as the China Youth League) is a youth organization for those between the ages of 14 and 28. It is run by the CCP and organized on the party's hierarchy pattern, with a central committee, national representative conference, and committees at various levels. The current CCP chairman, Hu Jintao, served as first secretary of the CCYL in 1984–1985. At the end of 2006, the CCYL Central Committee reported that the youth organization had 73.5 million league members, of which college and high school students accounted for 49.9 percent.

The ACFTU is the largest trade union in the world, with 134 million union members in 1.7 million primary trade union organizations as of 2005. It is divided into 31 regional federations and 10 national industrial unions. The party-controlled ACFTU facilitates government policy, not necessarily the protection of workers' rights. It has a monopoly on trade unionizing in China, and creating competing unions is illegal. This restriction on labor activism, combined with an increasing number of labor disputes, means that more and more workers are pressing court claims related to their work problems.

The CCP increased its membership from 2.7 million in 1947 to 6.1 million in 1951, and to 10.7 million by 1956. In this way, Mao rebuilt Chinese society through a party-state system that ended the 2,000-year-old clan/family-centered community that had previously protected individual lives. This traditional family value system was replaced by a political moral code based on loyalty to the Communist Party and Mao himself.

The 1949 Common Program had failed to protect the rights and liberties of the people under the new regime. In 1952, to deal with the increasing complaints, Beijing promised to formulate an official constitution based on the Common Program. Later that year, the Standing Committee of the CPPCC decided to create a national people's congress through general elections. At its forty-third session, held on December 24, 1952, this body agreed to commence the drafting of a constitution. On January 13, 1953, a committee for this purpose was established, and a draft was unanimously approved on June 14, 1954, at the Thirtieth CPG Plenary Session, and a revised version was discussed and approved by the Thirty-Fourth CPG Plenary Session. The Chinese government then attempted to create an official framework of central tasks of the country during this transitional period in the mid-1950s and to regulate the country's strides toward first socialism and then communism.

THE FIRST CONSTITUTION, 1954–1966

On September 20, 1954, the First National People's Congress (NPC) passed the first formal constitution by secret ballot and promulgated the Chinese Constitution. This document included a preamble and was divided into 106 articles in four chapters, much like the Soviet Union's constitution of 1936, which can be regarded as a civil law system. Parts of the Soviet legal code were directly translated into Chinese, and Russian legal experts also assisted in rewriting the code to better fit conditions in China. The 1954 Constitution included the president as the chief executive, the State Council as the executive body, the NPC as the main legislative body (a unicameral parliament), and the courts and procurates as the judicial branch.

The NPC elected Mao Zedong as the PRC's president on September 27, 1954. In April 1959, Mao stepped down as head of state, keeping his other powerful positions as chairman of the CCP and of the Central Military Commission. After Mao's resignation, Liu Shaoqi was elected as the PRC's second president, where he remained in office until—even though he could not legally be removed from office—he fell victim to the pressures of the Cultural Revolution (1966–1976), the largest and longest mass movement in the PRC's history. The constitution failed to protect even the president of the republic, and Liu died under house arrest in 1968.

Legislation and Elections

According to the 1954 Constitution, the National People's Congress was the highest state body and only legislative house in China. Until the 1990s, the NPC's representatives were determined by the CCP, which maintained effective control over the composition of the body at various levels. Each village could elect its own representative, with no restriction on the number of candidates, as the lowest level in the electoral system. Only this representative could enter the next level as a candidate to become the town or city congressional representative.

After the approval of the party committee of each town or city, each elected official could then enter the county-level election. At this level, the CCP exercised additional control over the process by limiting the number of candidates in proportion to the number of seats available. At the election of the county's people's congress (there were some

2,861 counties and county-level administrations in 2004), a maximum of 130 candidates was allowed per 100 seats. Following the approval of the county's party committee, each elected representative could serve a five-year term and enter as a candidate at the district election.

The next level after the district was the provincial election. Here, the ratio was 120 candidates per 100 seats. Delegates who were reelected by the provincial people's congresses could then enter the election for the National People's Congress. At this highest level, the ratio decreased again, to only 110 candidates per 100 seats. This tiered electoral structure made it impossible for a candidate to become a member of a higher legislative body without party approval. In 2000, more than 3,000 delegates attended the NPC.

According to the 1954 Constitution, the NPC exercised most of its power on a day-to-day basis through the Standing Committee in Beijing. Due to its overwhelming majority in the Congress, the CCP had total control over the composition of this committee. Until the late 1980s, the NPC and its Standing Committee played only a symbolic role as a powerless rubber-stamp legislature. They followed the Party Center's instructions and made sure to pass all of the party's decisions at the congressional meetings. All the local governments at the provincial, district, county, city, and town levels served as agents of the central government in Beijing. During the 1990s, the NPC and people's congresses at local levels began to play a new role, discussing their own issues, making their own decisions, and departing from the Party Center's agenda. But there is still a long way to go before the National People's Congress can play a separate role as an independent legislature in the Chinese government.

Judicial System

As a result of party control, the legal system was highly centralized. The 1954 Constitution authorized the Standing Committee of the NPC to select, appoint, and dismiss judges, procurators, and judicial personnel at the national level. Under the constitution, the standing committees of the provincial, district, county, and municipal people's congresses would appoint and dismiss the judicial personnel at the local levels. Local procuratorates were responsible to a similar body at the next higher level. Nevertheless, all the local judges, court clerks, and even police were hired and paid as the "cadres of the national government."

From 1954 to 1957, the NPC made some efforts to complete the country's legal system by drafting important legislation, including a criminal code. In 1954, the NPC created the Ministry of Justice, and that same year, the body passed five additional laws, establishing a general structure for state organs and legal institutions. These organic laws related to the NPC, the State Council, local people's congresses and people's committees, the people's courts, and the people's procuratorates. The Supreme Court became the highest judicial organ of the state, and Dong Biwu was elected as its first president, serving from 1954 to 1959. When Dong became the vice president of China, Xie Juezai took his seat until 1965.

In the meantime, a state law codification commission was created to establish the first criminal code to describe liability in detail. The commission published a series of documents for law enforcement and the assessors system. According to the new rules for the proper conduct of police, certain areas of police control were decentralized to local party committees throughout the 1950s. In 1955, the Ministry of Public Security of the PRC granted local party committees authority to manage the public police chiefs at their level. After 1958, local party committees became the main leaders of law enforcement in their areas.

Additionally, "Rules for Selecting People's Assessors" was issued by the Ministry of Justice in 1956. The people's assessors system was a type of adjudication mechanism for civilian participation in China's judicial justice. It is similar to the employment of "lay judges" in some European countries, such as Sweden and Germany. It was a copy of Soviet legal practice, which had some functional resemblance in the role of jurors from the Western common legal tradition. In 1963, China's Supreme Court issued a statement entitled "Announcement on the Election of People's Assessors through General Election at the Grassroots Level." These rules, however, were not followed until 25 years later.

Between 1954 and 1966, to cope with the new judicial establishment, law schools and legal publications became popular, with lawyers beginning to practice and citizens receiving encouragement to be law-abiding. In 1956, the Eighth National Congress of the CCP confirmed the importance of a strengthened legal system.

Party leaders, however, believed the legal system should serve, rather than restrict, the power of the CCP. Checks and balances were nonexistent; the government was not able (nor willing) to correct itself through the system, and the mass media were merely a mouthpiece of the Party Center. None of the liberties in the constitution were actually implemented. Article 89 of the constitution theoretically protected individual rights by guaranteeing freedom of speech, freedom of demonstration, and freedom of religion. These civil and political rights, however, were severely limited in practice or entirely canceled out by other articles, by constitutionally prescribed duties, or by other legislative acts. More and more intellectuals became concerned about the issues and problems inherent in the 1954 Constitution.

Anti-Rightist Movement

Between 1954 and 1956, the tension mounted between the specialists and the cadres, who were more concerned about Communist ideology than the legal system. The intellectuals also questioned the 1936 Soviet Constitution since Joseph Stalin never intended to grant the Russian people freedom, liberties, or fair trials. In 1956, Mao called for the "Blooming of the Hundred Flowers" movement to encourage the Chinese people, especially the intellectuals, to express their grievances on the mistakes, corruption, and mismanagement both in the government and in the party. When the criticism spread like a wildfire across the country, though, the chairman decided to stop the complaints by launching, in 1957, another political movement, the "Anti-Rightist" campaign.

The Anti-Rightist movement targeted nonparty members and those who were not interested in Communist politics. In schools and the mass media, party committees and branches mobilized the masses to identify "rightists"—meaning enemies of the people—among faculty members, researchers, and educated employees who might have said something bad about the government or the party during the Blooming of the Hundred Flowers movement. By the end of the year, more than 550,000 intellectuals had been labeled as rightists. Many of these individuals were purged and denied the right to work, teach, or live with their families. A large number were exiled to labor camps or remote villages for reeducation, and numerous others were jailed or executed. The accused received no respect for their human decency, let alone their rights and liberties. A whole generation of artists, scientists, journalists, educators, and even college and high school students were penalized. Three middle school students who spoke out against a party secretary in their school were shot to death in the presence of 10,000 people, including their teachers and classmates.

During the Blooming of the Hundred Flowers, several legal experts, lawyers, and judges identified problems in the legal system, such as the party's power abuses by overruling court decisions, excessive use of force by police, and violations of civil rights. Subsequently, in the 1957 Anti-Rightist movement, all of them, including four judges on the Supreme Court, were accused of using the law to oppose the party.

Thereafter, the PRC government consistently circumvented the constitution and the legal system in Mao's continued mass campaigns to eliminate any opposition. The reputation of legal institutions, including the courts and procuratorates, fell drastically, and lawyers began to stop practicing. The number of law schools was reduced from 83 to 12. The Ministry of Justice was closed in 1959, not to reopen until 20 years later, in 1979. Political security was a major concern for Chinese intellectuals and legal professionals from the late 1950s through the 1960s. Many young and middle-aged legal experts left the judicial system, which was considered as a sensitive and dangerous field. The fear factor of Mao's harsh, endless political campaigns against intellectuals worked.

The Great Leap Forward and People's Communes

In 1958, the Chinese state further expanded into all levels of society through Mao Zedong's Three Red Banners movement, including the General Line of Socialist Construction, Great Leap Forward, and people's communes. The campaign instated a bold advance on a large scale. All the industrial production targets for the second five-year plan (1958–1963) were doubled, and agricultural production targets were raised by 20 to 50 percent.

In rural areas, most peasants were organized into communes that controlled their productivity and distribution. Private land ownership and independent farming were nonexistent. Every peasant worked with others in a team and, through collective production, shared the annual yields. Under the people's commune system, peasants could not leave their units. If they wanted to travel, permission from village cadres was required; without receiving a certificate and food tickets from these officials, they would not have the necessary economic resources or legal permission. Transporting and selling goods from one place to another was regarded as speculation and profiteering, which were considered illegal activities. Furthermore, the markets in rural areas were banned as cradles for the petty bourgeois economy.

In the urban areas, residents were similarly denied freedom of movement without permission. Factory workers could not change or quit their jobs and were dependent upon their work unit for everything—food, medical care, housing, their children's education. The state controlled all the resources necessary for manufacturing, transportation, trade, banking, education, and social welfare. In 1958, tens of millions of people were mobilized in a nationwide movement of steelmaking, an extremely costly operation in terms of labor, capital, and raw material. Traditional craftsmen were all forced to participate in collectivized firms. Local officials, judges, and policemen were essentially agents of the central government.

China had become a state based on the complete control of all resources by the party-run government. The Great Leap Forward's consequences were even more disastrous than those of earlier programs. Many people's communes plunged into agricultural disaster. The grain harvest was dismal, leading to the widespread famine of the "three hard years," 1960–1963.

In the early 1960s, all the organizations of state power that had extended their reach into local communities underwent dramatic transformation. In the wake of the three hard years, the economic, political, and legal systems continued to diverge from Mao's ideal path of socialist construction. Mao also found that, to stabilize post-famine China, he had to stabilize his position within the party. In September 1962, he announced the slogan "Never Forget Class Struggle," at the same time accusing various people within the party and the government of disagreeing with his views.

"GREAT CHAOS UNDER THE HEAVENS," 1966–1976

Cultural Revolution and the Red Guards

By the mid-1960s, critics began questioning Mao's radical policies, including the Great Leap Forward and the people's communes, as well as other actions by the party and government. Mao responded to this opposition from pragmatist leaders with a new effort to mobilize support beyond the party by including students and the masses. This movement became the Great Proletarian Cultural Revolution. In the summer of 1966, the Cultural Revolution became a nationwide political struggle accompanied by extensive purges. Mao used mass organizations such as the millions involved in the Red Guards to publicly attack President Liu Shaoqi and the party's secretary-general, Deng Xiaoping, whose loyalty Mao questioned.

The Red Guards, mostly college, high school, and middle school students, were empowered by the chairman and became the driving force for this new movement. In the middle of 1966, all grade schools and colleges dismissed classes and allowed students to participate in the Cultural Revolution. Coming out of the schools, tens of millions of Red Guards blanketed the land in terror with a wild spree of home searches, property destruction, free-for-all fights, and even murder. The restriction of liberties reached new heights, and religious activities were prohibited. Respect for the basic rights of decency, let alone human rights, were nonexistent for those targeted by the Red Guards. According to revolutionary logic, one showed the proper commitment to class struggle by behaving inhumanely and cruelly toward other classes. Many Chinese lost freedom of employment, movement, and even marital life. The CCP and the Red Guards interfered with the private lives of the people, and speech and behavior were monitored by relatives, neighbors, and colleagues. Individuals had to report to Red Guard organizations on their private and even sexual relations. This system is sometimes termed "total institution."

In early 1967, as the Cultural Revolution began to overtake even the power of the authorities, the situation across the country worsened considerably. The Red Guards took over government offices at all levels, jailed the officials, and administered provincial and local affairs. Different factions within the youth organization, however, had contradictory political orientations and plans, leading to violent

The Red Guards parade an official through a Beijing street and force him to wear a dunce cap as a mark of public shame. He is a member of an anti-revolutionary group and, according to the writing on the cap, he has been accused of being a political pickpocket. This picture was taken in Beijing on January 25, 1967, and was obtained from Japanese sources in Tokyo. (AP Photo.)

conflicts within the movement, oftentimes resembling civil war. In July, for example, an armed clash took place between two different local mass organizations in Hubei and brought the entire province into a conflict in which more than 180,000 civilians and soldiers were killed or wounded. During these early years of the Cultural Revolution, from 1966 to 1969, an estimated 100 million people were killed, injured, or persecuted and victimized.

The legal system was also attacked during this period, as many existing government mechanisms were totally paralyzed. Most judicial officials and legal experts were removed from their positions by the Red Guards, who physically attacked many judges, procurators, lawyers, policemen, and court employees, including Xie Juezai, president of the Supreme Court. They were considered counterrevolutionaries within the government and accused of preventing the masses from joining the new revolution. The CCP's official newspaper called for lawlessness, with many articles denouncing the rule of law as a bourgeois form of restraint placed upon the people. The masses were encouraged to behave and act using Mao's Thought instead of the law, and slogans such as "Smash the Public Security, the Procuratorates, and the Courts" encouraged the attacking of legal institutions. The Soviet legal constructions previously incorporated by the Chinese were attacked as revisionist.

Military Control

In order to prevent civil war, Mao employed the People's Liberation Army (PLA) to restore social and political order through military administration at all levels of the government, including the schools. From 1967 to 1972, more than 2.8 million officers and soldiers participated in the replacement of civilian governments at the central, provincial, regional, county, and city levels through military administrative committees. The armed services also took control of the mass media, law enforcement, transportation, and all other pivotal activities and numbered more than six million troops altogether in 1969.

In 1970, the Cultural Revolution took an unexpected turn. A new political struggle erupted between Mao and Marshal Lin Biao, the defense minister and Mao's official successor. The two individuals differed in strategy, as well as foreign and domestic politics. For instance, when Mao proposed that the PRC constitution be amended to eliminate the post of head of state, Lin made a counterproposal that Mao assume the presidency. Angry and disappointed, Mao considered the marshal's ambitions and personal influence in the military dangerous and decided to take countermeasures. Lin and his family realized that Mao was directing his political struggle against them and that, after Liu and Deng, they would be the next victim of the chairman's brutal Cultural Revolution. Lin's son therefore planned to assassinate Mao on his way back to Shanghai, but when the plot failed, the family fled China by airplane for the Soviet Union on September 13, 1971. For unknown reasons, the plane crashed in Mongolia, and Lin, his family, crew members, and others on board were all killed in the crash.

After this incident, Mao began another top-down purge and shakeup in the military, continuing the Cultural Revolution until his death in Beijing in September 1976.[3] In October, the Maoist leaders, known as the "Gang of Four," including his widow, Jiang Qing, were arrested and purged from the Party Center by pragmatic leaders such as Ye Jianying.

The 1975 Constitution

Before Mao's death, the second PRC constitution was adopted by the Fourth NPC at the First Plenary Session on January 13, 1975. It was promulgated in the midst of the unrest of the Cultural Revolution and contained only 30 articles, in stark contrast to the hundreds included in the 1954 Constitution. It had a completely rewritten preamble, which was consistent with the times, and ended with a slogan to struggle for new successes. Article 2 stated that the CCP was the leading force of the Chinese people. It also integrated the state constitution with the Communist Party by stating that the PLA was under the command of the Central Committee of the CCP. Radical terms such as "dictatorship of the proletariat," "social imperialism," and "proletarian internationalism" could be found in many places in this second constitution.

The 1975 document minimized or completely eliminated the courts and procuratorates. It did not retain individual rights such as that of freedom of speech and press; as in the first constitution, these rights were only for those loyal to Mao and the CCP. Nevertheless, the new work drastically reduced the institutionalized and systematic violations of human rights. After 1976, the human rights and civil liberties situation in China began to improve.

The 1975 Constitution was replaced with a new work in 1978 as the next generation of CCP leadership took control.

OPENING UP AND CRUSHING DOWN, 1977–1989

After his third return to the Party Center, Deng Xiaoping led the second generation of the CCP. He was intently focused on putting China on the road to prosperity by deprogramming Mao Zedong's system and convincing the people that economic reconstruction should be the first priority of the country after 10 years of the

Cultural Revolution and turmoil. Deng defended the market economy, declaring that it did not contradict socialism but was simply an economic tool that could serve any ideological cause. In Deng's system, Marxism and Mao's Thought became means to support the reform rather than an end that the party should attain.

The 1978 Constitution

In order to start his reform movement, Deng urged the National People's Congress to work on a new constitution. At the Plenary Session of the Fifth NPC on March 5, 1978, the third PRC constitution was promulgated. It doubled the number of articles, from 30 to 60, and contained another new preamble. Two years after the downfall of the Maoists, most notably the Gang of Four, the new constitution restored the courts and procuratorates. It also reinstated some of the citizens' rights, such as that to strike. For the first time, the new constitution stated that Taiwan was a part of China and that it must be liberated by the PRC, thus finishing the great task of reunifying the motherland. In 1979, the government added an amendment that dropped the "liberation" stance toward Taiwan and opted rather for peaceful reunification.

Since the 1978 Constitution was adopted just two years after the Cultural Revolution, it still carried some radical language, such as "Revolutionary Committees." It required support for the leadership of the CCP, and participation in the socialist system remained a component of citizens' duties. The new constitution did not create legal norms, and noncompliance with the document's provisions was common. For example, the cadres and law enforcement still acted extralegally. More than 10,000 cases of violations of personal rights—especially illegal searches and detentions, extortion, and confessions coerced by torture—were discovered and prosecuted by the procuratorates.[4]

The 1978 Constitution would be replaced four years later during Deng's era of reform.

Economic Reform

The market economy has dramatically changed the structure of Chinese society, especially in rural areas. After 1978, the concept of Mao's people's communes weakened considerably. Deng was the first

Communist leader to encourage people to become wealthy. With his slogan "To Be Rich Is Glorious," he won the people's support, most prominently in rural areas. Chinese peasants were determined to improve their living conditions, and they often succeeded, directly leading to the collapse of the entire commune system and the state's substantial retreat from rural society.[5]

Long-dissatisfied peasants started to redistribute the land to households on the condition that each would submit a certain amount of output to the government. This practice immediately achieved great success because, once again, individual farmers gained complete control of their inputs and outputs. The practice was also officially accepted nationwide after a short pioneering experiment in select areas and was then promoted as the "household production responsibility system" in 1979. The production contracting system simply gave peasants the right to control production, but potential redistribution of land prevented them from leaving their village, resulting in a decline of interest in serving in the military. An agricultural family needed as many household members as possible in order to receive a larger piece of land, and parents sought to keep their sons on the farm to succeed in the new competitive market. In the early 1980s, with a sizable portion of land in able hands, some of the peasants in the southern provinces quickly became wealthy, achieving an annual income of around $3,000, compared to a national peasant average of $60.

Social stratification in China manifested itself as a new challenge to the government. Since the late 1970s, economic reforms had improved the food supply to the cities and abolished the food rationing (or quota) system for urban residents. Economic growth somewhat diminished the boundaries between different social statuses that had been clearly and rigidly marked in the past. The loosening of government control over people's mobility and movement further allowed farmers to take up occupations originally available only to urban residents. All of this helped to diversify the homogeneous group of farmers into different social groups and quickly boosted a considerable number of them into a higher income stratum.

One feature of the social strata in the 1990s was the rapid polarization of wealth. Another striking feature of China's social change was the mobile or "floating" population. As the old apparatuses of migration control became less effective, rural people began to move spontaneously to urban areas without obtaining government approval. By the late 1990s, approximately 48 million individuals had successfully completed this transfer. As many as 110 million rural laborers were estimated to be on the move seeking work in cities in the first decade of the twenty-first century.

The "Democracy Walls" versus the Great Wall

As a result of the massive population movement, reforms eliminated one restriction on individual freedom after another. The strong desire for civil liberties has made almost all Communist control mechanisms obsolete. Freedom became increasingly available in both the workplace and the market economy. Despite the significant breakdown of limits on individual freedoms such as those of employment, movement, relocation, and retirement, the development of these liberties has not been balanced. In some important aspects, they were severely restricted, particularly in political expression.

In the fall of 1978, the democracy movement, sometimes called the "Democracy Walls," began to take hold in several major cities, including Beijing and Shanghai. Some workers, students, and city residents used posters, underground newsletters, and handwritten pamphlets to call for political reforms and democratic changes. In Beijing, posters covered the walls at the intersection of the Avenue of Eternal Peace and Xidan Street, near to Zhongnanhai, the residential compound of the CCP leaders. Hundreds of people began to gather at these walls everyday to paste new posters that criticized past party policies, hold discussion groups, and give speeches to the crowd.

At first, the Party Center, particularly reformers under the leadership of Deng Xiaoping, who were at the time trying to unite power against the more conservative Maoists, tolerated and even encouraged the movement. The next spring, however, the views on the walls expressed by some of the activists challenged the Four Basic Principles. Wei Jingsheng, a young electrician working at the Beijing Zoo, for example, posted a critique of Deng's Four Modernizations on the wall at Xidan Street, calling for a "fifth modernization": democracy.

At this point, even the party's reformers began to fear these new critical stances and political demands and believed they might threaten the country's stability and established modernization programs.

Confrontations escalated between the authorities and activists as the latter were asked to stop their postings. The struggles to save the Democracy Walls were dubbed the "Beijing Spring." Finally, the government took a series of steps to hold back the movement, including arresting the participants in larger cities and sentencing the leaders to lengthy jail time. Wei Jingsheng was arrested and received 15 years in jail.

In March 1979, in response to the Democracy Movement, Deng insisted on upholding the Four Basic Principles, which included keeping the country on the socialist road, upholding the people's democratic dictatorship, maintaining the leadership of the CCP, and following Marxism-Leninism and Mao's Thought. In June 1980, the Four Basic Principles were officially incorporated into the CCP Resolution as a historical document, and in 1982 they were included in the new constitution.

The 1982 Constitution

A market economy based on competitive production requires the stable rule of law in areas such as commerce, contracts, labor relations, and bankruptcy. A sound, reliable legal system is essential, not only for bringing basic efficiency to the domestic economy, but as a requirement of international investors and those who participate in the country's other commercial activities. This economic imperative pressured the second generation of CCP leadership to engage in numerous legal reforms, including the revision of the 1978 Constitution.

To prepare a new constitution, a Committee to Amend the Constitution was established on September 10, 1980. It completed a draft version in February 1982, which was then submitted to the NPC Standing Committee for national discussion. On December 4, 1982, the Fifth Plenary Session of the Fifth NPC adopted the new document by secret ballot.

The 1982 Constitution was the longest such document in the PRC's history, containing 138 articles. It represented a mix of continuity and change compared to the previous versions. Many sections of the current document were adapted directly from the 1978 Constitution, while some new concepts and articles were added. For example, the 1982 Constitution states that class struggle is no longer the top priority for the country and people; it places economic development and improvement of the people's standard of living as the top priority. It also affirms the idea of legality and other related concepts, expressly stating that the party must operate within the scope of the constitution and law. It does, however, stress that any exercise of rights or freedoms is unconstitutional and unlawful if it violates any of the Four Basic Principles enshrined in the preamble to the document.

The 1982 Constitution has four chapters, including "The Fundamental Rights and Duties of Citizens." This chapter contains a complete, detailed, and elaborate list of rights, unlike the constitutions of 1954, 1975, and 1978. Some of the new provisions in the latest version were specifically designed to avoid the civil and human rights violations of the Great Cultural Revolution in the 1960s. The chapter also lists several fundamental rights and duties of citizens that were enacted after the constitution was ratified.

After 1982, the legal system was revived in China, and many law schools reopened again. More and more textbooks and legal magazines were published, and lawyers once again began to practice. The courts handled more cases than at any time in the past, with more than 2.5 million reported in 1986.[6] The Ministry of Justice was reestablished under the State Council, as well. In public discourse, slogans such as "Rule the Country by Law" have been increasingly used.

The 1989 Tiananmen Square Incident

The magnitude of China's social transformation carried within itself seeds of instability. During the 1980s, new problems emerged. Official corruption, abuses of power, and the theft of public property were rampant in spite of the government's efforts to control them. The reforms accentuated the sharp disparities that existed between the rich and poor. To ensure stability, instead of improving civil liberties, Deng insisted on the Four Basic Principles: keeping to the socialist road, upholding the people's democratic dictatorship, maintaining the CCP's leadership, and adhering to Marxism-Leninism and Mao's Thought. Nevertheless, increasing political dissatisfaction, highlighted by antigovernment minority revolts, prodemocracy activities, and widespread complaints of corruption among party and government officials challenged Deng and other Chinese leaders.

In April 1989, prodemocracy student activities on Beijing campuses became citywide and then turned into national demonstrations demanding political reforms across the country and protesting against corruption and power abuse. The government's negative attitude and harsh condemnation caused more dissatisfaction, among not only students but also the rest of the population. In May, hundreds of thousands of students and citizens joined together and held demonstrations at Tiananmen Square—Beijing's equivalent of the Mall in Washington, D.C., or Red Square in Moscow—which had become a traditional site for popular protests since the May 4 Movement in 1919. From the capital, the demonstrations spread to 116 cities across the country. On May 6, the Beijing students encamped at Tiananmen Square for 10 days and began a hunger strike to show their determination in promoting democracy and ending corruption. Rather than engaging the students politically, the Party Center decided to employ the PLA in a law enforcement role to deal with the activists.

The People's Liberation Army is China's armed forces, including the army, navy, air force, and strategic missile defense, and totaled 3.5 million troops at the time. PLA soldiers are responsible for guarding military facilities, and each city has a garrison command that is responsible for maintaining order among off-duty PLA soldiers and PLA vehicles in transit. The local garrison will post small groups of soldiers to patrol the streets and check military vehicles; however, these patrols do not get involved with or interfere in the public security duties of the local police forces. In Beijing, PLA soldiers perform guard duties in and around Tiananmen Square at Mao's Mausoleum, the Great Hall of the People, and the leadership compound of Zhongnanhai. In the 1989 Tiananmen Square incident, however, the armed forces played a major role in crushing the prodemocracy student movement.

On May 19, the CCP established martial law in Beijing and ordered a large number of PLA troops to move into the city, including 22 infantry divisions from 13 PLA armies. This attempt to restore order was not effective, however, so the Party Center prepared for a final crackdown. After initial clashes between the troops and citizens in Beijing, the CCP leaders called an emergency meeting on June 3 and decided they were confronted by a "counterrevolutionary riot" that would have to be put down by force. That evening, troops forced their way through the streets, followed by tanks and

A Chinese man stands in front of tanks heading down Chang'an Boulevard, past the Beijing Hotel, near Tiananmen Square, China, June 5, 1989. The tanks stopped their advance momentarily as he cried and pleaded for an end to the killing in China's capital. The man was pulled away by bystanders and the tanks continued. (AP Photo.)

armored vehicles. Early the next morning, about 1:00 A.M. on June 4, the troops clashed with some of the citizens and students, who tried to stop the troops from entering Tiananmen Square. An estimated 1,000 students were killed, while both city residents and PLA troops also suffered casualties. By 7:00 A.M., the troops had ended the protest and occupation of Tiananmen Square.

As a result of the massive use of armed force against civilians, the problem of civil liberties and human rights became a serious crisis, which undermined Deng's reform movement.

After the Tiananmen Square incident, Western countries joined in all-out condemnation of Beijing's military suppression of the student-led movement. Most Americans supported President George H. W. Bush's response, which suspended official bilateral exchanges with China and participated in economic sanctions imposed on China by other Western industrial countries. Deng, however, continued his economic reform, with a new philosophy of "building socialism with Chinese characteristics." Health problems soon reduced his political role, though, and Deng died a few years later in Beijing, on February 28, 1997.

LEGAL REFORM, 1997–2009

Following Deng's departure from power, the new third generation of CCP leadership recognized that the authoritarian power structure and secretive policy making had helped create the crisis of 1989. Accordingly, the new government officials began to avoid arbitrary policy construction and unpredictable risk in the 1990s. The political and economic imperatives made it more desirable for the new leader, Jiang Zemin, to develop more consistent and procedural policies through legal reform.

Inadequate laws and their selective enforcement had seriously undermined the market economy and stunted the state reform movement. In the mid-1990s, cronyism was rampant and corruption had been accepted as a necessary tool in loosening the machinery of the government. The new administration intended to cut off old-guard connections and get rid of past problems by normalizing the legal system and establishing new regulations. It saw the rule of law as the only mechanism that could provide an underlying structure upon which the free market could take hold, thereby pushing China toward becoming a more modern state.

Concurrently, the Chinese people became more aware of their rights as citizens. Much of Chinese society increasingly demanded legislative and adjudicative due process and the general protection of their rights from the interference of the state. In 1997, Jiang, then chairman of the CCP, called for the rule of law at the Fifteenth CCP National Congress. By the late 1990s, China was on course toward real legal reform.

Judicial Independence

In 1999, the Chinese Supreme Court issued its first five-year plan for reforming the country's courts. It addressed problems such as competence, fairness, judicial training, and regularity in court procedures. The plan embraced some important reforms, such as the creation of rules regarding the use of evidence and the separation of cases from adjudication, and adjudication from enforcement. Since then, the legal profession has become increasingly institutionalized, marked by an expansion in legal education and an increasing awareness on the part of the citizenry as to their rights under the law.

As a result of this reform, the legal system has been somewhat depoliticized. A discourse on the legitimization of the law has developed in society, primarily from the bottom up. The courts slowly evolved from simply serving as political tools for the campaigns of the past to providing justice in individual cases. Many judges now wear robes, in contrast to the military uniforms that were previously worn, and increasingly wish to have their courts separate from other branches of the party-state. Court discussions and decisions have changed from enforcing party policy to being neutral in order to resolve disputes. The new requirements for the selection of judges reflect a change from a primary reliance upon their political backgrounds, instead focusing on members of the judiciary who have significant professional experience.

The changes in the courts signify the decentralization of the party-state in the 1990s. During the political turmoil of the late 1980s, the judiciary had not been a challenge to party authority, and on the contrary contributed to the local stability and social order which the Party Center desperately needed. The influx of the Internet and other communication technologies has made political control outside party channels more difficult. This development, among others, has challenged the party leadership, as the centralized government was supposed to solve the problems that accompanied a move toward capitalism. Instead of successfully addressing these issues, however, the situation has created new class divisions and a new set of problems, proving again that the cure can sometimes be far worse than the disease. The Party Center has a dilemma: either it must give up some power to local control or risk losing control altogether, making the former a necessary transformation. The center, however, lacks both the ability and the inclination to monitor its local agents in a uniform manner across all sectors, thus assuring that law enforcement remains distanced from the party apparatus.

As a result of these legal reforms, the courts have become increasingly used for rights-based litigation. In 1999, the courts handled six million cases, five million of them civil, which is more than double the number heard in 1986. In addition, more than 10 million letters were sent to courts, accompanied by a corresponding increase in visits.[7] The strengthened institution has also enjoyed an increase in power as the courts enhanced their supervisory function. Like the police, the courts answer to local government in most cases. Although they are not yet to the standard of those in Western countries, the increasing role of the judiciary is in itself a significant development. In 2000, for the first time, over 20 percent of Chinese judges had college degrees, up from just 6 percent in 1995.

Law Enforcement

China has one of the largest law enforcement workforces in the world. According to official statistics from 2007, the PRC has more than 580,000 police officers and 150,000 detectives and investigators, all of whom are under the control of the Ministry of Public Security in Beijing. This ministry has a bureau of public security in each province and county, a metropolitan police department in each city, and precinct offices in each district. In 2003, this top-down centralized police system had 31 provincial bureaus of public security, 356 metropolitan police departments, 2,972 county police headquarters, and 41,941 local police stations. There are also more than 250,000 traffic cops, street patrollers, and special police, and some cities even have anti-riot units. Estimates of the total complement of China's law enforcement forces may vary, but are usually in the vicinity of one million and rising.

As a general rule, police officers in China do not perform static guard duty, but are tasked with controlling the population, fighting crime, and maintaining safety. Police officers patrol on foot or in vehicles, and they operate out of small, interconnected command boxes on the city streets. Some urban centers have anti-riot units equipped with a few armored cars. Previously, those involved in law enforcement went unarmed, but since late 1994, circumstances have required them to carry sidearms more often. The official Chinese newspaper reported in 1996 that more than 300 police officers had been killed every year since 1993.[8] In January 1996, new rules were issued concerning the use of batons, tear gas, handcuffs, water cannons, firearms, and explosives. These regulations updated the 1980 guidelines and were a response to the rise in crime.[9] Despite these new adjustments, police forces are not considered part of the armed forces of China as defined by the *National Security Law*. Police officers have a system of ranks, with insignia composed of triangles, diamonds, and gold leaves.

Aside from the state police force, private and collective security guards assist in law enforcement, particularly at the entrances to many factories, construction sites, residential areas, hotels, sports arenas, and civilian businesses. Usually, they are hired from a private company and receive a limited amount of specialized training. These personnel, estimated in 1993 to number around 200,000, are often demobilized soldiers of the PLA or itinerant workers from the countryside and cities. Their uniforms are an assortment of PLA pieces, which vary from company to company and may look very similar to those used by state forces. While they may have a whistle and flashlight, they are generally unarmed and, in their mission to control access in and out of their area of responsibility, would notify local police forces in case of an emergency. They often refer to themselves as "public security," and are sometimes given the nickname of "rent-a-cops" by foreigners. They have no official relationship with the Ministry of Public Security, the PLA, or the People's Armed Police.

The People's Armed Police

As part of the legal reforms, China strengthened the People's Armed Police (PAP) in the 1990s. This national organization was established in 1983 and is made up of regular troops, something like a combination of the National Guard and police SWAT (special weapons and tactics) teams in the United States. In late 1996, the Chinese government transferred 14 infantry divisions of PLA regular soldiers, totaling 150,000 men, to the PAP force. By 2000, the PAP was composed of one million members.[10] As of 2003, the PAP had 31 armies, including 508 armed police regiments and 42 helicopter, artillery, tank, chemical, engineering, and transportation regiments. The PAP also had 32 command academies and 29 hospitals across the country.

While the People's Liberation Army focuses on external defense missions, the People's Armed Police is charged with maintaining internal stability. The transfer of army divisions to the PAP was an example of the senior Chinese leaders' desire to avoid using the military to enforce social order. The PRC Law on National Defense, adopted on March 14, 1997, describes the chain of command and defines the mission of the PAP. Article 22 reads, "Under the leadership and command of the State Council and the Central Military Commission, the Chinese People's Armed Police is charged by the state with the mission of safeguarding security and maintaining public order."[11] The new law, however, is not clear about how the force may be ordered into action. Article 6 states that the local government may request the use of the PAP:

> Local people's governments at various levels and locally stationed military organizations may call joint meetings, when necessary, to coordinate the solution of problems concerning national defense in their respective administrative areas . . . and matters shall be separately reported by them to higher authorities.[12]

The duties performed by the PAP in the routine maintenance of internal security are considerably different from those of the police. In addition to guarding their own facilities, the branch's troopers perform several standard public security missions: standing guard at important bridges and government and party buildings, safeguarding foreign diplomatic areas, and ensuring the protection of senior leadership. Additionally, they participate in street patrols, carry out ceremonial duties, and, as mentioned previously, back up the police forces. Usually, PAP members are conscripted during the same recruiting period observed by the PLA, and which branch a new recruit enters may be nothing more than the luck of the draw. New members of both forces undergo very similar basic training, and because many of their soldiering skills overlap, such as marching, driving, and small arms practice, the PAP uses many of the same regulations and manuals as the army. The more advanced techniques for each branch, however, are considerably different. By maintaining a strict differentiation between the missions of the two forces, both are better able to concentrate on their primary roles.

A frequent topic of interest on internal Chinese television news is police–PAP cooperation in making drug busts and combating smuggling. In some situations, the police appear to be in charge of making the arrests, while the PAP troopers remain in the rear prepared to provide reinforcing muscle if necessary. In many cities throughout the country, these two organizations jointly patrol the streets, conduct roadblocks, and make the accompanying searches. At particularly sensitive times and locations, members of both forces will dress in civilian clothes to lower their profile as they monitor the situation, and, if necessary, swarm to control an incident they deem potentially dangerous. Both have the primary objective of containing any disturbance, no matter how small, before it grows out of control.[13]

The 14 divisions that were transferred from the PLA to the PAP have been busy since 1997. Just in 1997, for example, in addition to assisting the police in fighting crime, two divisions of the PAP were deployed in Xinjiang to deal with disturbances in Yining. Other units were called in to the South Korean embassy in Beijing during an incident involving a North Korean defector. Several regiments were sent to the Wuyun district in the southern province of Guangdong to end a dispute over an administrative boundary change. On July 8–10, 1997, the PAP was called in at Mianyang, in the city of Chengdu, to cope with demonstrations that had arisen from the closing of state-run textile plants and involved 100,000 people. That fall, the PAP was sent to Beixiang, in Guangdong province, to restore order after approximately 1,000 farmers fought with local officials and police because of alleged underpayments on grain they had brought to the market. Later that year, the PAP marched into the streets of Dujiangyan, north of Chengdu, to deal with nearly 1,000 laid-off workers who had surrounded government offices. Before the end of the year, a company of the PAP rushed to southwest Guangzhou, Guangdong province, where several dozen villagers who were protesting the one-child policy threw stones at policemen. With the exception of the incidents in Mianyang and Xinjiang, where two Muslims were killed during the riots, the branch did not use deadly force in any of these crises.

Law as a Tool to Govern

The late 1990s and early 2000s were years of extraordinary changes in China's legal system. A high degree of continuity, however, remained from previous periods of rule and constitutions, especially in the area of civil liberties and people's rights. These problems and China's excuses can be clearly seen in government documents published by the State Council, such as "Progress in China's Human Rights Cause" (March

1997), "Freedom of Religious Belief in China" (October 1997), "New Progress in Human Rights in the Tibet Autonomous Region" (February 1998), and "National Minorities Policy and Its Practice in China" (September 1999).[14] During this time, the country faced new challenges as well as old problems, such as human rights violations, suppression of religions and political dissent, abuse of prisoners, and women's rights. The PRC's conduct in these fields remains a top concern for the U.S. government, which has pledged to support intensive efforts to promote freedom in all countries. The challenges facing China require serious political will and new resources. The Chinese government must interact with all its citizens and civil society groups in ongoing legal and political reforms.

From 2003 to 2009, the Chinese government sped up legal reform by adopting new legislation, including labor laws, public records regulations, and military statutes. Among other important military legislation, in December 2003, the CCP's Central Military Commission adopted new regulations on the subject of "Political Work of the People's Liberation Army."[15] The Communist Party maintains control of the military by channeling the military elite's interests and the individual consciousness. In February 2004, the Central Military Commission released "Provisions on Strengthening the Education and Management of High- and Middle-Ranking Officers of the PLA," and in April, it issued new regulations entitled "Work of the CCP Armed Force Committees." These new rules reflected the confidence of the Party Center in the existing strong political institution. Since the state has adapted well to economic and social changes and effectively responded to the rising demands and expectations of the PLA, its political institutions should be able to manage some of the discontent and differing opinions within the PLA in the near future.[16]

Although the Chinese government had made some progress in its legal reforms in the first decade of the twenty-first century, international organizations and rights groups noted that China was promising a lot, but had delivered little. On March 6, 2007, the U.S. Department of State issued its annual report on Chinese people's rights and stated that the condition of human and civil rights in China "remained poor." On July 29, 2008, Amnesty International titled its report on the subject: "China: The Olympics Countdown—Broken Promise." The UN Human Rights Council in its "Universal Periodic Review" on February 9,

2009, concluded that the country had a long way to go for the protection of its people's rights and civil liberties. The U.S. Congressional Executive Commission on China reported online publicly on 734 cases of jailed political dissenters and religious leaders in China.

On New Year's Eve in 2009, British prime minister Gordon Brown condemned the Chinese government decision to execute a British citizen in Xinjiang. Akmal Shaikh, the British man, was convicted of smuggling drugs from Tajikistan to Xinjiang and sentenced to death in October 2009. Despite the British government's request and his family's appeals for clemency on the grounds of mental illness, Chinese authorities executed him by lethal injection on December 29, 2009.

To understand the Chinese policy and government behavior, it is necessary to have a close look at their political, judicial, and social institutions to explain the ongoing events and problems.

Chapter 2

Sound Is Better Than Silence

This chapter examines the place of the freedoms of speech, political expression, the press, association, assembly, peaceful demonstration, and political dissent in contemporary China. It provides a balanced view that includes an examination of both official efforts to protect constitutional rights in the past years and current inhibitions and limits to progress and further improvement. The chapter identifies some major factors behind the nation's continuing problems in these areas and explains why the 2010–2020 decade will be crucial for the development of civil liberties in the PRC.

The country has reached a crossroads in development that will continue and consume the next decade. China's low production costs and export-oriented economy reached their apogee in 2008, and the next year saw a substantial slowdown in the growth of its economy. To offset this setback, the government must deal with the social and political issues that have arisen in the past two decades, largely as a result of rapid economic expansion, such as labor relations, unemployment, inflation, social stratification, a damaged environment, corruption, and organized crime.

China is in the midst of a momentous transition, and more and more of the nation's people are demanding greater government accountability. They reject the increasing human cost that has accompanied this "economic miracle." Many of them, including 700 million rural inhabitants, an estimated 150–200 million migrant workers, and more than two million former employees of state-owned enterprises, have lost their jobs, homes, access to basic health care, and an affordable education for their children. The unemployment rate has increased to 9 percent in recent years. In most cases, however, the government continues to ignore the issues and cover up the problems by ensuring a lack of public voices, media criticism, and legal liability. The Chinese legal system has failed to protect the freedom of speech and provide judicial supervision. According to the annual reports released by the U.S. Department of State, the U.S. Congressional Executive Commission on China, Amnesty International, and Human Rights Watch, the condition of civil liberties in China remained poor in 2008.

With almost 1.4 billion people, the challenges facing China are enormous and complex and require new efforts in legal and political reforms. Despite provisions in the Chinese constitution that protect the freedoms of speech, association, privacy, and communication, a clear gap exists between the law and reality. The government has little tolerance for criticism or calls for greater transparency and account-ability, and instead emphasizes the need for a harmonious society and political stability during the economic recession. Beijing continues to restrict some of its citizens' fundamental rights and employs the law enforcement and legal system to suppress political dissent, unregis-tered organizations, and unauthorized activities.

This chapter examines some specific incidents when reporters, acti-vists, and intellectuals have criticized government policy or organized some association or demonstration in China during the first decade of the twenty-first century. Their stories present a small window into the struggles endured by the Chinese people as they try to speak out and demand accountability and responsibility from those in power.

RIGHTS AND IMPROVEMENT

In the present constitution, promulgated in 1982, the second chap-ter, entitled "The Fundamental Rights and Duties of Citizens," lists protected civil rights.[1] Article 35 declares, "Citizens of the People's Republic of China enjoy freedom of speech, of the press, of assembly, of association, of procession and of demonstration." Article 40 states:

Freedom and privacy of correspondence of citizens of the People's Republic of China are protected by law. No organization or indi-vidual may, on any ground, infringe upon citizens' freedom and privacy of correspondence, except in cases where, to meet the needs of State security or of criminal investigation, public security or procuratorial organs are permitted to censor correspondence in accordance with the procedures prescribed by law.

In Article 41, there are much more detailed and elaborate protections of the rights for citizens to criticize the government than are in the corresponding parts of the previous constitutions. Obviously, some of the provisions in the present constitution are specifically designed to prevent civil and human rights violations that took place in the Cultural Revolution and other political movements during Mao's era from 1950 to 1976.

Among other rights, the constitution pledges the citizens' right to equality before the law; political rights to participate in elections; and some personal freedoms. Even though the constitution also promises some social and economic rights, the Chinese government always locates civil and human rights issues within this category: feeding the largest population in the world is China's fundamental human rights issue, which is a different perspective from that in the West. The PRC government has been able to save the nation, where a liberal or democratic government might have been too ineffective and weak to do so. Nonetheless, after 1982, Beijing continued to show more improvements in the civil liberties and human rights legislation:

- In April 1988, the First Session of the Seventh National People's Congress adopted two constitutional amendments: one on private property and the other on protection of the ownership of the private property.
- In March 1993, the First Session of the Eighth NPC made nine important amendments, including some changes in the preamble to the constitution.
- In March 1999, the Second Session of the Ninth NPC adopted and published six constitutional amendments for enforcement.
- According to an official report, in 2003, the Central Committee of the CCP proposed amendments to the Constitution that included the phrase: "The state respects and guarantees human rights."[2]
- On March 14, 2004, the Second Session of the Tenth National People's Congress adopted and published 14 amendments to the constitution. Among the most important changes was the addition

of the Central Committee's phrase to Article 33: "The state respects and guarantees human rights." This marked the first time the Chinese constitution mentioned human rights, and, according to the government, it indicates that respecting and safeguarding these issues is no longer limited to party and government policy, but is an ideal enshrined in the fabric of the nation and critical to the progress of the state.

However, in 2003, the government revised the Publications Administration regulations and the Regulations Governing the Administration of Audio-Visual Products to put increased stipulations on the previously mentioned freedoms. The Publications Administration's regulations state that "citizens may, in accordance with these Regulations, freely express in publications their opinion and expectations of state affairs, economic and cultural undertakings and social affairs, and freely publish the results of their scientific research, literary or artistic creations and other cultural pursuits."[3]

According to the official annual report, the Chinese government has promoted the press, allowing encouraging circumstances in which citizens can enjoy their freedoms. This new vigor on the part of the press has had a significant impact on the development of democracy in the country, especially as citizens can now, for the most part, talk about the government privately. The democratic development has begun at the local level for peasants and villagers. Among the 34 provinces, autonomous regions, and centrally administered municipalities, twenty-eight of them have implemented the Organic Law of Villagers Committees, and 31 have organized village election committees. The average rate of participation in the elections is 80 percent, and it exceeds 90 percent in Guangdong, Hainan, Sichuan, and Hunan provinces.

Although Western scholars do not yet believe China is a democratic society, most will agree that the freedom of speech for its citizens has dramatically improved. However, on some issues, individuals in the country are required not to violate the Four Basic Principles of the constitution, a requirement that in itself is a restriction on the freedom of speech.

China claims that it has given top priority to the people's lives, health, and basic human rights. An official Chinese human rights report published in March 2004 professed that the government has adopted an attitude of "holding itself accountable to the people, acting in their interests, and accepting their supervision." The government was furthermore said to have formulated the following principles of governance: "governing the country for the people" and "using the power for the people, sharing the feelings of the people and working for the interests of the people."[4]

To showcase these efforts, the Chinese government has adopted some measures for respecting and safeguarding political and human rights. In 2005, the Chinese government promised to release many political prisoners who had been jailed since 1989 in order to curb worldwide criticism and win support for its Olympic Games bid. After the International Olympic Committee voted Beijing to host the 2008 Summer Olympics, the Chinese government continued to show improvement in protecting political and human rights in China. In 2006, for example, China continued to allow local villagers to elect their village chiefs through democratic and open elections; more than 500 million villagers voted at the 624,000 villages across the country. In 2007, the government issued new regulations to allow the foreign media for the first time to film local events and interview Chinese citizens. In 2008, especially during the Beijing Olympic Games, more efforts were made by the Chinese government in this direction. Many China watchers and international rights groups, however, still believe that the Chinese government has not done enough to improve civil liberties and human rights conditions in the country.

RESTRAINTS AND CONTROL

The limits and problems of China's civil liberties protection can be identified in legislative, executive, and judicial procedures. First of all, the 1982 Constitution stresses in its preamble that any expression of rights or freedoms is unlawful if they violate the Four Basic Principles: namely, to keep the country on the socialist road, uphold the people's democratic dictatorship, promote the leadership of the CCP, and follow Marxism-Leninism and Mao's Thought. Moreover, a citizen's exercise of his or her rights and freedoms cannot conflict with the state's interests or other citizens' rights.

In the existing laws, the restrictions on freedom of speech primarily come from Article 51 of the constitution, which stipulates that "citizens

A pro-democracy activist has her mouth taped to symbolize Chinese government restrictions on freedom of speech. She carries a Chinese flag with a black ribbon tied to it (top) at the start of a protest outside a venue where a flag-raising ceremony was taking place in Hong Kong, to mark China's National Day and the 50th anniversary of the establishment of the People's Republic of China on October 1, 1999. (AP Photo/Anat Givon.)

of the People's Republic of China, in exercising their freedom and rights, may not infringe upon the interests of the State, of society or of the collective, or upon the lawful freedoms and rights of other citizens." In addition, speeches may be judged according to the provisions of criminal law, including such charges as of antirevolutionary propaganda, insults, slander, and false witness. Similar restrictions on speech can be found in civil and administrative law. Thus, the Chinese government can easily restrict the freedom of speech and the press wherever it wants to link them to the jeopardy of national, social, and collective interests.

Turning to the executive branch, following the constitutional restrictions on civil liberties, the Chinese government continues to issue more regulations to limit citizens' rights. The State Council makes administrative rules and regulations to restrain the freedoms of speech and of assembly. For example, after the Tiananmen Square incident in June 1989, the State Council on October 31 issued the Act on Marches and Demonstrations, limiting citizens' rights to assemble, march, and demonstrate. According to this Act, before citizens organize an assembly, march, or demonstration, they must first apply for permission from the authorities (clause 7). The application would be disapproved if, in the opinion of the authorities, the assembly, march, or demonstration opposes the fundamental principles of the constitution; if national unity, sovereignty, or territorial integrity are threatened; if a national split is advocated; or if enough evidence is garnered to prove that the planned event would directly endanger public security and seriously disturb social order (clause 12). In addition, the Act also stipulates that "citizens cannot initiate, organize, or incite citizens of cities outside the organizers' home cities to participate in the assembly, march, or demonstration" (clause 15). Furthermore, "Those who work in government offices must not organize or participate in the assemblies, marches, or demonstrations that violate the duties and responsibilities stipulated by laws or regulations for government officials" (clause 16). And, "The time for assemblies, marches, and demonstrations is limited to the period from 6:00 A.M. to 10:00 P.M." (clause 24). Another example of restrictions on the freedom of speech is in the Act on Guarding State Secrets. This administrative act enumerates 17 categories of state secrets, encompassing, in effect, almost anything not publicly released.

Finally, Chinese judicial procedures also allow the legislature and legal system to restrain freedom of speech and freedom of the press. The Chinese legal system is different from other civil law systems. The PRC constitution does not systematically outline general principles that all administrative regulations and rules must follow. Instead, each governmental branch is capable of setting up its own guidelines, while the principles of legislation are listed in the basic laws carried out by the National People's Congress and its Standing Committee. The provincial governments also make their own laws. Local laws and regulations are issued by the provincial, city, and county governments, as well, even though all of these ordinary laws are in theory incorporated with those at the national level.

The way in which civil liberties can be compromised can be illustrated by examining the freedoms of speech, publication, and "procession." The Criminal Law, for instance, was adopted by the NPC's

Standing Committee in 1979 and amended in 1997 due to an increase in crime throughout the country.[5] This body of legal provisions provides the "principal punishments," including criminal detention, fixed-term imprisonment, life imprisonment, and the death penalty. Under some criticism, it provides a category of "counterrevolutionary offenses," such as antigovernment propaganda or other acts that "endanger the People's Republic of China" and are "committed to the goal of overthrowing the political power of the dictatorship of the proletariat and the socialist system."[6]

Additionally, because the legal provisions for the freedom of speech are incomplete, the liberties of citizens can be restricted administratively. There are extralegal restrictions, which include those enacted by government agencies, leaders, moral judges, and party policy, none of which are legally binding. These limits are primarily imposed on public criticism, complaints, and suggestions.

What is especially crucial is government control of the mass media, which ensures that voices critical of the state will not be heard. The authorities have organized huge institutions and related networks charged with duties, such as monitoring speeches, to reach this end. A censorship system has been adopted for news of great importance, which must be issued only by appointed authoritative bodies and not by private media outlets. Controversial political topics may be discussed individually or in small groups, but if a speech that includes controversial material is made publicly or is disseminated to overseas audiences, those involved may be—and often are—punished.

POLITICAL EXPRESSION: "DARE TO PUBLISH IT"

Currently, the freedoms of speech and of the press are restricted in both legal and extralegal ways. Laws stipulate that when citizens are exercising these stated rights, they must obey the constitution and not jeopardize national, social, or collective interests. Those who want to speak out are often charged by authorities with violating the legal rights and freedoms of *other* citizens.

Take, for example, Dr. Gao Yaojie, an 82-year-old physician who was fighting the spread of AIDS in the countryside when she was named to receive the Human Rights Award from an international women's organization in the United States in the summer of 2006. At the awards ceremony, Dr. Gao criticized Chinese policies and the lack of health care in rural areas. After her return to China, she was placed under house arrest for "violating the rights of other citizens." In September of the same year, Yang Chunlin, a peasant representative in Jiamusi, in northeastern Heilongjiang province, met with local officials and demanded compensation for peasants who had lost their land to urban development. He was arrested by police and charged with "inciting subversion of the government." In Hangzhou, in southeastern Jiangsu province, Yang Yunbiao complained publicly about the city government's forced relocation of residents. He was arrested and sentenced to two years' imprisonment. Facing the denial of their right to freedom of speech, more citizens, both urban and rural, are beginning to demand that the authorities respect and enforce their constitutional rights.

In the meantime, more and more journalists, writers, and intellectuals are also calling for the protection of the freedoms of speech and the press. These groups make up the core of the political struggle for individual and corporate freedom of political expression. In China, most news agencies, media companies, publishers, book retailers, and libraries are owned and managed by the central or local governments. The authorities control the resources, market, and audience with a strict media censorship. Thus, the press is simultaneously regarded as the voice of the Communist Party, the government, and the people.

In January 1997, the State Council placed restrictions on publications, particularly their scope, while at the same time granting the freedom to publish. These regulations list in detail many of the prohibitions on the media, extending to areas such as printing, copying, and distribution. For example:

> The units that conduct printing or copying of publications can begin their business only after they apply to the executive agencies of the province, autonomous region, or municipality where they are located for approval and register their business with public security agencies and administrative agencies of industry and commerce. (clause 31)

Books and articles that address sensitive areas of the party and government are frequently suppressed. The Department of Propaganda in the CCP Central Committee sets up the guidelines and issues the party's instructions on a regular basis to the media, telling them what news to report and how to phrase it. The Xinhua (New China) News Agency, acting as the party's mouthpiece, releases the official version of the news for the other news agencies, newspapers, TV, radio, and magazines to follow. The General Administration of Press and Publications (GAPP) in the State Council has the authority to screen, censor, and ban any print or electronic publication in China. It does so by controlling the publishing licenses and quotas, such as International Standard Book Numbers (ISBN) and International Standard Serial Numbers (ISSN). The GAPP can also recall books, destroy printed journals, or even shut down a publishing house. In late 2004, a wave of detentions reflected a new campaign targeting writers, journalists, and political commentators.

Frequently, conflicts between the central government agencies and local media, as well as between publishers and writers, arise because of the undermining of the freedoms of speech and the press. Zhang Yihe, for example, a retired Peking Opera researcher, wrote a historical book entitled *Stories of the Opera Stars*. It relates the stories and legends of the opera singers who suffered during the Cultural Revolution of the 1960s. Since the book addresses some sensitive areas of history and criticizes the ruling party, it appears on a list of books that are banned for publication. The Hunan Literature Publishing House nevertheless printed the book in 2006. On January 11, 2007, on the opening day of a national conference for the industry, the GAPP called a meeting between publishers and officials of the agency. A GAPP deputy director admonished the group: "We have reminded you repeatedly about this person. Her books are not to be published. . . . You dared to publish it." The GAPP penalized the Hunan Literature Publishing House by cutting the number of books approved for it by around 150. In the past, this would have marked the end of the story, but in this case, Zhang became one of the first authors to complain publicly that the regime had stifled her constitutional right to freedom of expression. During an interview with Radio Free Asia (RFA), she said: "If my books had been banned under a transparent system with all the due process and probity of the law, then I would respect that. But that's not what happened here."[7]

The party and government have recently begun to share their authority with the courts. In 2008 in Fuyang, in southeastern Anhui province, a former county party secretary brought libel charges against two authors, whose work *Survey of China's Peasants* discussed the lives of local peasants. In their controversial book, the authors gave a heart-rending account of the abuse and hardships suffered by Anhui farmers at the hands of corrupt local officials. After the work was published by Beijing's People's Literary Publishing Company, it sold millions of copies and sparked intense debate in Internet chat rooms and bulletin boards. In the past, the county government would simply have arrested the authors and burned their books, charging them with anti-government or counterrevolutionary actions, but in this instance, the former local official submitted a libel suit to the Fuyang Intermediate People's Court. On June 23, 2009, police arrested Liu Xiaobo, a writer and political dissident, in Beijing. In December, the Beijing Supreme Court sentenced Liu to 11 years in prison because of his "inciting subversion of state power."

ORGANIZED VOICES AND POLITICAL DISSENT

China does not have special laws that protect citizens' freedom of association and freedom of demonstration. Presently, the Administrative Regulations on the Registration of Social Organizations, issued by the State Council in 1989, still apply. This Act has many restrictions on the freedom of association. It stipulates that social organizations can conduct activities only after they are approved and registered (clause 2) and continues:

"Social organizations must abide by the constitution, laws, regulations, and support and defend national unity, as well as the unity of different nationalities. They cannot jeopardize national, social, and collective interests and the legal freedom and rights of other citizens" (clause 3). The application for the formation of a social organization must be "reviewed and approved by the agencies that are in charge of the affairs concerned and be registered in the agencies responsible for registration" (clause 9). In practice, citizens' applications are generally not approved because of the restrictions of these regulations.

By 2008, there were 387,000 registered citizen social organizations in China, including 3,259 legal aid organizations. All active and approved social organizations are sponsored by concerned government agencies, not individual citizens. Most of them cannot engage in basic activities such as fund-raising, membership drives, or disaster relief. Many of the organizational directors, board members, and secretaries require official approval after their election. Therefore, the right of association is very weak at best. On the other hand, it cannot be denied that the emergence of many of these groups in recent years has improved collective and individual freedoms.

Authorities continue to harass and arrest those expressing political dissent, despite sometimes flexible policies. In March 2004, the Chinese government released dissident Wang Youcai in response to repeated requests by the U.S. government. Wang had been serving an 11-year sentence for founding a would-be opposition party, the China Democracy Party. Before the NPC national convention, he was released from the Zhejiang Provincial No. 1 Prison and allowed to travel to the United States on medical parole. In March 2006, the Chinese authorities released Tong Shidong, a 72-year-old political dissident, before President Hu Jintao's visit to the United States. Tong was a retired physics professor in central Hunan province who was first arrested in 1999, then again in 2002, and was finally sentenced to six years in jail in June 2005 for helping to organize the China Democracy Party. "It's the way of the Chinese government in dealing with dissidents," Szeto Wah told an RFA reporter. As the chairman of the Hong Kong Alliance in Support of Patriotic Democratic Movements in China, Wah explained: "They arrest them and use them as hostages. Then they release them when some issues are coming up. This time may be related to the visit of Hu Jintao to the U.S. There is no loosening of restrictions on freedom of speech in China. Controls are still very tight."[8]

In May and June 2007, authorities arrested some members of the Pan-Blue Alliance, which recognized the Chinese Nationalist Party in Taiwan and promoted the Three Principles of the People.[9] Because of its political orientation, the alliance could not get registered and became an illegal organization. Most of its leaders were arrested or sent to the labor camps or mental hospitals, while its websites and newsletters were shut down by the government.

The authorities, if they believe it necessary, bar political dissidents from going overseas or returning back home. On February 9, 2007, officials at Beijing International Airport refused to allow Zhang Yu, a political dissident, to reenter the country. Zhang was returning from a conference of the International PEN writers' group in Hong Kong.

As the general secretary of the Chinese writers' group, he had been critical of the government's censorship policies. Despite arguments that it was illegal for a country to turn away its own citizens, such things happen in China, often based solely on verbal orders from high party officials. Many Chinese are denied permission to leave the country to participate at international conferences, as well. For example, more than 20 Chinese writers were prevented from attending the International PEN meeting in 2007.

Some Chinese journalists, lawyers, intellectuals, and activists who raise issues of official corruption, public health, and environmental crises face persecution, prosecution, harassment, detention, and torture. Individuals who attempt to form an independent trade union or engage in non-state-approved associations have been sentenced to long jail terms and even to death. Aside from the legal stipulations, the government's restrictions on citizens' assemblies, marches, and demonstrations are also reflected in the procedures of the public security agencies. Because of the ambiguity and broad nature of the twelfth clause of the Act on Marches and Demonstrations, applications for assembly, marches, and demonstrations are not usually approved.

In recent years, demonstrations have increased against city and county governments that are involved in illegal land seizures, mismanagement, forced evictions, corruption, violation of civil liberties, and the abuse of power by local officials. Demonstrations take different forms, from the traditional petitions to mass incidents that involve a large number of participants. The petition remains a popular form of protest, with those utilizing it seeking to bring public complaints against local officials to those higher in the administrative hierarchy, often in order to resolve grievances such as corruption, forced relocation and resettlement, and misadministration. Larger events include protests, demonstrations, and sometimes riots.

According to the official statistics of the Ministry of Public Security, there were 58,000 "mass incidents" in 2003 and 74,000 in 2004.[10] In 2005, the country experienced 87,000 mass protests, an average of one every five minutes. In December 2005, thousands of local farmers and fishermen joined together and protested the inadequate compensation they received for land confiscated for the construction of a power plant. Police and People's Armed Police (PAP) forces moved in and crushed the demonstration, killing between 10 and 20 villagers. These crackdowns usually result in arbitrary arrests, torture, and a general atmosphere of terror. Following a decrease in 2006, the authorities have stopped disclosing figures concerning the number of riots and demonstrations.[11]

In 2007, all 34 province-level governments reported large-scale demonstrations. Several of these involved tens of thousands of people. On March 13, 2007, for instance, the city residents in Yongzhou, Hunan province, protested a bus fare increase that was reportedly caused by the city government's mismanagement and corruption. By March 15, more than 20,000 people gathered in the streets and boycotted public transportation. The government refused to lower the bus fare, and instead sent 2,000 armed police and declared martial law in the city. Many protesters were attacked by the armed police and several dozen were arrested.

In many cases, authorities have continually denied people their rights to hold peaceful demonstrations. In early 2007, the government of Xiamen, a major city in southeastern Fujian province, began construction of an aromatic paraxylene chemical plant, about 10 miles from the city center. The 11-billion-yuan-*Renminbi* (RMB, Chinese currency) chemical plant would produce 800,000 tons of paraxylene per year. The city residents, about 1.5 million in total, worried about pollution from the chemical plant and began to express their concerns in May. With no reply from the city government, protests began on June 1 with more than 10,000 people, demanding the termination of the construction. The protesters broke through police roadblocks and arrived in the front of the city hall. The clash between the protesters and police brought many injuries to both sides.

Some officials even encourage mobs to attack the people who held a demonstration or a strike. In July 2007, a group of workers in Heyuan, in southern Guangdong province, held a strike around their factory, protesting not having been paid for four months. Officials organized a group of 200 strikebreakers, armed with spades, axes, and steel pipes, who attacked the striking workers, killing one worker and causing many serious injuries.

In the northwestern Xinjiang Uyghur Autonomous Region (XUAR), authorities have used the global war on terror as a pretext for harshly cracking down on suspected Uyghur separatists who were expressing peaceful political dissent. As one of the minority groups in China,

A Uyghur man walks past armed police officers standing guard in Urumqi, in western China's Xinjiang province on July 9, 2009. Security forces kept a firm grip on the tense Xinjiang capital after days of ethnic violence that killed 156 people, and alarmed Chinese leaders vowed to deal firmly with those behind the attacks. (AP Photo/Eugene Hoshiko.)

Uyghur people comprise 45 percent of the XUAR population. Chinese officials began a campaign in the region focused on three problems: extremism, separatism, and terrorism. The government at both the provincial and local levels, however, was often unable or unwilling to identify and distinguish between those who were terrorists and the members of peaceful activist and religious groups, resulting in many raids and arrests of those participating in religious worship and nonviolent protest. Tensions mounted between Uyghurs and Han Chinese people, who make up about 40 percent of the XUAR population. In 2008, there were several waves of protest in the region. On July 5, 2009, more than a thousand Uyghur demonstrators gathered in the commercial center of Urumqi, the capital city of the XUAR, protesting the government's handling of the death of two Uyghur workers and demanding a full investigation of the killings. After confrontations with police, the peaceful demonstration escalated into riots on July 5–7. PAP and city police used tear gas, water hoses, and armored vehicles to attack the demonstrators, while the XUAR government imposed a curfew in Urumqi. The riots continued when hundreds of Han people clashed with both police and Uyghurs. According to the government reports, 197 people died and 1,721 others were injured during the two-day riot.

The problems and restrictions mentioned in this chapter constitute the final barriers that citizens must break down in order to enjoy their freedoms of speech and assembly. The Foreign Affairs Committee of British House of Commons concluded in its 2007 Human Rights Annual Report that there was only "glacial progress" in China's effort to guarantee people's civil liberties and human rights. In 2008, eight U.S. Congress members proposed House Resolution 610, demanding further improvement of civil and human rights conditions in China and threatening a U.S. boycott of the Beijing Olympic Games.

The Chinese government used to rebut Western criticism of its constraints on the freedoms of speech and assembly. However, in recent years, Beijing has acknowledged that the country has significant problems in the area of political rights and civil liberties protection. Nevertheless, the government also argues that these issues can be addressed through the current political system. It insists that it will take time, since any push for fundamental change brings the risk of instability and a breakdown of economic development. These barriers are the last remnants of the Communist system of repression and persecution, and the gradual and substantive expansion of liberties in these areas will undoubtedly pave the way for China's democratization. By getting the state out of these areas of sociopolitical life, Chinese civil society will grow and flourish for the benefit of all, including the functionaries of the state. Thus, while encouraging the rule of law, these restrictions actually run counter to the principles embedded in the Chinese constitution. Without these liberties, the Chinese people will never reach their potential for creativity, happiness, and development.

Chapter 3

Faith and Freedom

In the past decade, China has seen a surge in the number of people turning to such religions as Buddhism, Islam, Protestantism, Catholicism, and Daoism (Taoism). As a result of rapid economic growth and sweeping social, ideological, and political change, more and more Chinese people are searching for meaning and emotional stability in their lives. According to the official statistics, in 2008, there were more than 250 million followers of various religious faiths. The Chinese government has become more tolerant of officially recognized churches, temples, and religious groups by pursuing a more flexible policy.

The Chinese traditional religions, without subscribing to a personalized God, brought considerable support to the government by giving supernatural sanction to the emperor or the ruling party. The ethical system of their religions reinforced traditional values such as loyalty, hard work, obedience, and sacrifice as an institutional system to maintain the ethical-political order. Now, however, as increasing numbers of Chinese people join religious groups for freedom of worship and demand a new order of equality, justice, and plenty, the ruling Chinese Communist Party and the government begin to limit freedom by banning the followers from participation in these religious activities.

The ultimate test of building a "harmonious society" in the 2010s rests on how the Chinese government handles freedom of religion and human rights. At the beginning of the second decade of the twenty-first century, the Chinese government uses a dual policy to maintain political control. Beijing allows organized religious groups and manages the transformational activities. Concurrently, the Communist regime continues to harshly crack down on any unofficial religious movements and activities that have a strong popular following, fearing that they might grow powerful enough to challenge party authority. Having transformed from a totalitarian government to an authoritarian one during the 1980s, China still has a long way to go to achieve a balance of social harmony and freedom of religion.

Between 1949 and 1979, the Communist government, following Marxist concepts, declared all religion to be deceptive, monstrous, and perverse. This definition was based on two arguments: first, that religion was a man-made illusion or, to use Karl Marx's phrase, the "opium of the people"; second, that it served as a tool through which Western imperialists and other dominating classes could gain spiritual control over Old China. Therefore, religion became an ideological issue for the new totalitarian government. After 1949, religious practice was condemned and, in most cases, prohibited. Many religious institutions and agencies, as well as adherents, were labeled "antirevolutionary," and their activities were claimed to be based on superstition and working toward espionage, both detrimental to the revolutionary cause. In the 1950s, many churches and temples were shut down and congregations dismantled, as the government followed policies of persecution. Naturally, religion became a major target of the Cultural Revolution, and during the Destruction of Four Olds campaign in the late 1960s and early 1970s, the Red Guards burned Bibles, tortured monks and nuns, and destroyed many religious institutions.

Since the 1980s, when the reform and liberalization movement began in China, the government has become more flexible and pragmatic in its policies concerning religious establishments. It has lifted the ban on religious practice and repaired some historic religious sites. Many Chinese people have embraced this new freedom, greatly enjoying the accompanying self-realization, intellectual expression, emotional potential, and search for spirituality. Some have begun to practice Buddhism, Islam, Daoism, or Christianity, either returning to their pre-1949 family tradition or exploring new spiritual sources. The government, however, continues to maintain a certain amount of control over religion by restricting numerous freedoms.

This chapter examines China's religious practices, the balance between freedom and denial of religious expression, and governmental interference with certain religious groups. It focuses on Christianity, Buddhism, and Islam, with an emphasis on certain regions such as

Xizang (Tibet) and Xinjiang, as well as specific groups, like the Falun Gong group.

RELIGIOUS EXERCISE

In the 1982 Constitution, freedom of religion is a basic right, guaranteed to all citizens. Article 36 stipulates clearly, "Citizens of the People's Republic of China enjoy freedom of religious belief." It goes on to say, "No state organ, public organization or individual may compel citizens to believe in, or not to believe in, any religion: nor may they discriminate against citizens who believe in, or do not believe in, any religion." Additionally, it declares, "the State protects normal religious activities." There are five officially recognized religions: Daoism, Buddhism, Islam, nondenominational Christianity, and Catholicism. Among other major religions are Confucianism, Moism, and Falun Gong.

Although the constitution recognizes that worship is part of a citizen's personal life, it requires respect for those who do not have a religious belief. Since the 70 million CCP members in theory do not have a religious belief, the Chinese government emphasizes that those who do have one must get along and cooperate politically with those who do not. The government also makes it clear that any religion in China should be adapted to its society and the reality that China is a socialist country. Thus, the government requires all religions in China to align their activities with socialist principles and government policies.

Under the constitution, governmental branches have issued many codes and regulations on religious practices in China. For example, in 2004–2005, regulations regarding religious affairs were published as parts of the Law on National Regional Autonomy, General Principles of the Civil Law, Education Law, Labor Law, Compulsory Education Law, Electoral Law of the People's Congress, Organic Law of the Villagers' Committees, and Advertisement Law. The government claims that these laws stipulate that all citizens, regardless of their religious beliefs, have their political, economic, and religious rights. Beijing believes that all of these legal protections of the citizen's right to freedom of religion are mostly in accordance with the main content of international agreements and conventions such as the UN Charter, the Universal Declaration of Human Rights, the International Covenant on Civil and Political Rights, the UN Declaration on the Elimination of All Forms of Intolerance and Discrimination based on Religion or Belief, and the Vienna Declaration and Action Program. However, some of the rules limit freedom of worship by restraining religious activities. For example, the State Council issued the Regulations on the Administration of Sites for Religious Activities and the Provisions on the Administration of Religious Activities of Aliens within the Territory of the PRC, administrative laws that put limitations on freedom of worship. According to these regulations, no religious group shall violate any of these rules, and no foreigner can attend religious rituals in China without approval by the governments at or above the county level.

Beijing instructs government and party officials from the top down to provide close supervision of the religious groups. The governments at all levels are to exercise effective control of religious activities by carrying out the party policies and reinforcing the governmental laws. Under the PRC State Council, the Religious Affairs Bureau acts as the central government's enforcement and management agency of religious affairs. Also, under the Chinese People's Political Consultative Conference (CPPCC), there is the Democratic Religious Council, which represents the major religious groups by receiving and housing their representatives in Beijing. In the meantime, the government has increased the number of officials who oversee and supervise religious affairs across the country. In the National People's Congress and the CPPCC, there are more than 24,000 governmental personnel who work on religious affairs.

To serve the quarter of a billion followers of various religions, China as of 1999 had more than 85,000 sites for religious activities, about 300,000 clergy, and more than 3,000 religious organizations. In addition, there were 74 religious schools and colleges run by ecumenical organizations for the training of clerical personnel. As the largest religion in the country, Buddhism has more than 80 million followers, with a total of 13,000 temples, including 3,000 Tibetan and 1,600 Pali structures. They house around 200,000 Buddhist monks and nuns, including 120,000 lamas and more than 10,000 Bhiksu and senior monks. Daoism, the next largest religion, has an estimated 45 million followers, over 1,500 temples, and more than 25,000 priests and nuns. Islam is third, with 35 million adherents. Their 30,000 mosques are served by 40,000 imams and akhunds.[1]

Presently, China has about 25 million Christians. There are some 5 million Catholics, with 4,000 clergy and more than 4,600 churches and meeting houses. Protestants total 20 million, including 18,000 clergy, and have 12,000 churches and 25,000 other meeting places. In an apparent attempt to contain the flood of new Christian converts, authorities in Beijing have built two new churches in the capital, the first since the Communist Party came to power in 1949. The Beijing Municipal Administration spent $4.8 million for the construction of these facilities, each of which accommodates approximately 1,000 congregants.[2] The city's Religious Affairs Office has stated that the city government will continue to endorse the officially recognized Beijing Municipal Christian Association.

Among the traditional religions, Buddhism, Islam, and Daoism not only are popular but also represent different ways of life and form many minority groups in China. At present, 55 minorities in the country have a total of 76 million members, approximately 7.2 percent of the country's population (the majority group is the Han Chinese, constituting 92 percent of the total population). Among the large minorities are the Mongolian, Hui, Tibetan, Uyghur (or Uighur), Miao, and Yi peoples. Tibetan Buddhists and Muslims form large minorities based on religious groups.

With a total population of three million, Tibetan Buddhists consist of the Tibetan, Moinba, Lhoba, and Naxi ethnic groups. All of these minority groups practice Buddhism and live in Tibet (Xizang), one of China's five autonomous regions set aside for ethnic minorities. According to official reports, there are more than 1,700 Buddhist temples in Tibet, and about 46,000 Buddhist monks and nuns live in these temples. Tibet also has other religious groups, including Muslims, Catholics, and Daoists.

The Chinese government has been involved in some of the major religious activities to show its "support" of these religions. Its involvement, however, has resulted in tension or even conflicts between the government and the religious groups, especially the Tibetan Buddhists. For example, in 1992, the State Bureau of Religions of the State Council in Beijing was involved directly with determining the lineage reincarnating the great lama of the Tibetan Buddhists. The State Bureau of Religions accepted the succession of the Living Buddha of the 17th Karmapa.[3] Thus, for the first time in Tibetan Buddhism, the

Chinese government was involved in choosing their spiritual leader, who will play a very important role in sustaining and developing Buddhist doctrines.

Ten minority groups are primarily Muslim, including the Hui and Uyghurs in Xinjiang. Xinjiang is a border region in northwest China and the hinterland of the Eurasian continent, covering approximately 550,000 square miles, or one-sixth of the total Chinese territory. Its population is over 20 million, including 12 million people from forty-seven different minorities, such as the Uyghur, Kazak, Hui, Mongolian, Kirgiz, Tajik, Ozbek, and Tartar peoples. It is another of China's five autonomous regions for ethnic minorities. Historically, in Xinjiang, the dominant religious group has changed over time, but the coexistence of multiple faiths has always been necessary. Along with the Muslims, the region has Buddhists (including Tibetan Buddhists), Protestants, Catholics, and Daoists. Most believers follow a faith along ethnic lines; for example, the Uyghurs, Kazakhs, and Hui believe in Islam. Xinjiang contains more than 24,000 venues for religious activities, of which the

The Id Kah Mosque in Kashgar in the Xinjiang Uighur Autonomous Region of China. This is one of the largest mosques in China. (Gayle Britt.)

vast majority are mosques. At the provincial level, there are 13 Islamic and three Buddhist movements, as well as one Three-Self Patriotic Movement Committee of the Protestant Churches. At the county level, the region hosts 65 Islamic associations, two Buddhist associations, and two Three-Self Patriotic Movement Committees.[4]

GOVERNMENT INTERFERENCE

While the constitution protects the freedom of religious belief, the government has placed many restrictions on this liberty. Policies demand that religious groups maintain the unity of Chinese people and protect the security of their country. In other words, the church and temple should not divide the people or separate themselves from the majority of the people. Their activities should not undermine the national security. Additionally, the constitution requires that "no one may make use of religion to engage in activities that disrupt public order, impair the health of citizens or interfere with the educational system of the state." Therefore, religious activity must conform to the regulations, interests, and safety of the state. In other words, religious activities should serve and protect national interests, not endanger or harm national unity. The government also uses the rationale of protecting the freedom *not* to have a religious belief, stating that this is a more complete and comprehensive protection of citizens' basic rights.

The ruling Chinese Communist Party has its own political considerations, since the CCP is still an atheistic party and must protect its political base. The party's members, numbering approximately 70 million at present, have not been allowed to practice any religion and are required to commit themselves to the atheistic revolutionary cause. They must actively advocate science and dialectical materialism to combat the stated absurdity of theism. Some party members privately violate this rule, but doing so openly would limit their political career and professional development.

The government maintains control of religious exercises through a registration process and national organizations. All theistic groups must be registered with the authorities, and all religious publications, personnel appointments, and seminary programs must go through a continuing official review and approval process. The church or temple can conduct only the government-approved worship and activities.[5]

Oversight is also empowered by top-down national organizations; for the seven officially recognized religions, these are the Buddhist Association of China, Daoist Association of China, Islamic Association of China, Chinese Patriotic Catholic Association, Chinese Catholic Bishop's College, Three-Self Patriotic Movement Committee of the Protestant Churches of China, and China Christian Council. All local groups must incorporate themselves into these national institutions. Additionally, teachings in these associations are monitored and sometimes modified by the government, which further scrutinizes their membership, financial records, and employees. The national organizations working as governmental agencies can deny any application for regional programs or local activities. Any activity, publication, or appointment that fails to register or to get approved may be subject to criminal prosecution, fines, and closure.

The government also maintains control through leadership choices. The Chinese authorities, for example, have the power to ensure that no new Living Buddha can be identified. After the Panchen Lama died in 1989, the search began in Tibet to locate the boy who was the reincarnation of the Panchen Lama and a new Living Buddha for Tibetan Buddhism. The Dalai Lama, the exiled spiritual leader of Tibetan Buddhism, followed Buddhist tradition and in May 1995 announced that the search had identified the eleventh reincarnation of the Panchen Lama. The Chinese government, however, denied the recommendation by the Dalai Lama in America.

The Dalai Lama has been in exile since 1959 when he was accused by the central government of organizing a separatist movement in Tibet by force. Chinese troops entered Tibet and suppressed the Buddhist rebellion in March 1959. The Dalai Lama then escaped into India. Over the past 40 years, the Dalai Lama and his government in exile have been campaigning for freedom of religion in China, criticizing China's violations of human rights, and demanding independence for Tibet. The Dalai Lama received the Nobel Peace Prize in 1989.

Having denounced the Dalai Lama's "interference" and "sabotage" in 1995, the Chinese government decided to involve itself in the naming of the reincarnation of the Living Buddha of the tenth Panchen Lama. Beijing adopted the method of a lottery to determine the reincarnated baby boy in Tibet. The new method had much more to do with defending the supreme authority of the central government than the continuity of Tibetan tradition. On November 29, 1995, a six-year-old boy was chosen at the lot-drawing in Tibet as the eleventh Panchen Lama, and the government of the Tibetan Autonomous Region reported its selection to the State Council for approval. Since this incident in Tibet, the government has issued a document entitled "State Administration for Religious Affairs," which includes 14 regulations designed to limit the influence of the Dalai Lama. Most notably, it declares that no "Living Buddha [may be reincarnated] without government approval."[6]

This type of attempted control over religious groups is not limited to Buddhism in China. The government does not allow any foreign involvement in Chinese religious activities without official approval; Article 36 of the constitution stipulates that religious organizations and affairs must be free from "interference by foreign forces," meaning that churches in China cannot be under any foreign control or influence. Additional regulations issued by the government prohibit foreign-based religious groups and individuals from organizing subgroups, setting up offices, establishing schools for religious purposes, or opening places for activities. The foreign churches cannot appoint their clerks, promote their religion, or conduct any activities in China without permission.

In the Catholic Church, priests and especially higher officials must take orders from the Vatican, which directly contradicts the demands placed on all clergy in China, who are supposed to follow instructions from the party. Because of this, many religious activists have asserted that the CCP is unlikely to ever allow direct ties between Chinese Catholics and the Vatican, which poses some bureaucratic problems.[7]

In 1998, the government barred outspoken Hong Kong Catholic bishop Joseph Zen from traveling to mainland China following a speech he gave in the Vatican that attacked the Communist country's lack of religious freedom. He repeated demands that Beijing release detained underground Catholic bishops and provide religious freedom to all to worship outside state-backed "patriotic" organizations. In April 2005, after Pope John Paul II died, China permitted officially sponsored prayers for the deceased, but refused to send an envoy to his funeral. In Beijing alone, close to 10,000 worshippers went to funeral masses that were held in five major Catholic churches. Officially sanctioned ceremonies were also held in Shanghai, Tianjin, and other major cities. When the Catholic bishop, Fu Tieshan, died in 2007, Beijing refused to accept a successor appointed by the pope.

THE "UNDERGROUND CHURCH" AND THE "EVIL CULT"

The growth of religious groups in China is tempered by state control and persecution. The state-approval system prevents the rise of groups that are not controlled by the government. Reprisals against unregistered groups have primarily focused on the Christians who, for various reasons, choose to attend "house churches" or "underground churches." Some Catholics remain loyal to the pope and the Vatican rather than to the Chinese Catholic Patriotic Association. The Vatican insists that it has ultimate authority over doctrine and the appointment of Catholic Church officials, while the Chinese government believes that this is interference in China's internal affairs. What has made Beijing even angrier is that the Vatican still maintains diplomatic relations with the Nationalist government on Taiwan. For these reasons, many Catholics choose to worship outside the state-controlled congregations.

Many new converts, especially Christians, worship at underground churches. Officially, there are about 5 million Catholics in China; however, according to the Vatican and other Catholic sources, the number is closer to 10 million, with half of them worshipping outside the state-managed churches.[8] The official number of Protestants is 18–20 million, but unofficial estimates indicate that there are more than 30 million Protestants in China today. Some of the underground Christian churches and congregations receive financial and spiritual assistance from overseas organizations and foreign religious groups.

The Chinese government dislikes having religious groups and activities outside the system, especially with connections to foreign religious groups, which they see as reminiscent of missionary work that accompanied past Western imperialist aggression against China. To prevent any further influence of the Western Christian churches, the State Council issued the Administrative Regulations on Religious Sites on January 13, 1994. The new statutes placed severe restrictions on family churches and individual religious activities. Thereafter, house churches and their members have faced tremendous difficulties in continuing their worship and programs and have sometimes been harassed by local government officials. Heavy fines are also common and often result in the confiscation of personal effects in lieu of a payment that is ignored or unavailable. Sometimes persecution takes the form of a prison sentence or "reeducation" through manual labor. The leaders of underground churches frequently face serious charges, including conducting "illegal business practices."

In early April 2004, for example, Xu Shuangfu (or Xu Shengguang), leader of a group known as the Three Grades of Servant, was abducted along with another prominent house church leader by unidentified individuals driving a police jeep. The Three Grades of Servant, or Church of Truth, is an unofficial religious group based in China's northeast and claims millions of followers. Some Westerners consider it to be an orthodox Christian house church network. The group had been targeted by authorities as an "evil cult," second only to the *qigong*-based Falun Gong, and Xu had previously been arrested close to 20 times. On April 27, police in northeastern Heilongjiang province raided some house churches of the Three Grades of Servant and arrested dozens of people. Among those detained was Gu Xianggao, a 28-year-old schoolteacher. Two days later, his family received a death notice from the police. His parents believe their son was beaten to death while in police custody. On July 7, 2006, the provincial court sentenced Xu to death and executed him immediately. The court also gave death sentences to three other church leaders with a two-year reprieve, which usually leads to a life sentence. Eleven church members received various sentences from 3 to 15 years in prison.

In May 2006, another house church leader, Zhao Wenquan, was detained in Mengcheng County in the eastern province of Anhui, and his house was searched. Reportedly, Zhao led more than 4,000 followers, and for this, he was charged with "illegal assembly and disturbing the peace." On December 7, 2007, police in Linyi, in the eastern province of Shandong, burst in on a Bible study meeting held in a house church, with 270 participants. The villagers had gathered as part of a fast to honor Jesus' suffering. Seventy of them were arrested, and several were beaten. Then, each person was told he or she had to pay 300 yuan RMB for the expenses incurred during their 15-day detention period. Police also confiscated their computers, video recorders, televisions, videotapes, and many copies of the Bible.

Yao Liang, a Catholic bishop of an underground church, became very popular in the northern province of Hebei. His weekly masses reportedly had more than a thousand people in attendance. Authorities arrested him in 2006 and sentenced him to many years in prison. On December 30, 2009, Yao died in jail. In 2007, authorities arrested 270 priests of the underground Christian churches. Twenty-one of them received prison sentences from one to three years. The other 249 priests were detained for a while and then released after each paid a huge fine to the government.

Nevertheless, house church leaders have not been officially outlawed, and the country has seen increasing official toleration. This decrease in persecution did not come about because of newfound support for Christian churches, but because of the concerns of the new Party Center, which sought to increase its own popularity. The government does continue to suppress larger and more popular religious groups such as Falun Gong, which is perceived as a threat to governmental authority and national stability.

Falun Gong was one of the exercise groups based on *qigong* (body energy control) established in China in May 1992. Li Hongzhi explained that the group's name means "Dharma Wheel Practice." Li called it Dafa, meaning "the Great Law," or Falun Dafa, the "Great Law of the Dharma Wheel." The group's practices include five sets of simple slow-motion breathing *qigong* exercises meant to increase health and spirit. Regular practice puts a "dharma wheel" into the lower abdomen, which believers can rotate to release energy for their needs. The ultimate objective of practicing Falun Gong is to "attain the *Dao*," or way of the Buddha. According to Li, Falun Gong, as one of the Buddhist Laws, could help those who truly seek salvation through a lifetime of commitment to the practice and eventually lead to their "consummation." In an interview in early 1999, before the government purged his group, Li told *Time* magazine that the group's practices "are primarily aimed at healing illnesses or keeping fit and maintaining good health. I am teaching a higher level of *qigong*." Furthermore, he said, it is meant to "eliminate your Karma, to remove your improper thoughts." The "Fa" should be "regarded as re-creation, which would mean discarding you completely and re-creating another person. . . . In the end they can free themselves from the worldly state."[9]

In the mid-1990s, the group spread into almost every province in China. It evolved into a religious cult with characteristics attractive to many Chinese, including the middle class, elderly women, and weak elements of society. Unemployed men joined it for health reasons, but found sympathy and support in the group. In 1997, Falun Gong claimed to have 100 million members, although the government put estimates at 10 million. The problems began when more and more CCP members participated in its daily practices and large assemblies, which were often held at city centers. The local party committees and governments tried to stop party members from participating and limited their exercise grounds. In 1997–1998, practitioners presented a number of appeals and petitions, but achieved negligible results.

On April 25, 1999, 10,000 members of Falun Gong gathered at Zhongnanhai, the residential compound of the country's top leaders, an action that finally led Jiang Zemin and the Party Center to persecute the group. The government banned Falun Gong on July 20 and declared it to be an unlawful "evil cult." On July 29, the authorities ordered the arrest of the group's founder and leader, Li Hongzhi. The party leadership then began a nationwide crackdown by mobilizing all the means of the government, including the police, army, media, state-owned enterprises, and schools. A large-scale propaganda campaign through newspapers and television denounced the Falun Gong as the enemy of the state and the people. Local police began to arrest Falun Gong leaders and active members, while the armed police and army used armored vehicles to crush their public rallies and demonstrations.[10] The organization estimated that nearly 90,000 members were arrested, 60,000 of whom were tortured in prison, and 3,000 died during or after their incarceration or forced labor.[11]

Following the 1999 edict, protests in the cities were frequent, but they have now been largely eradicated. From January to July 2008, for example, 586 Falun Gong members were arrested in the Beijing area alone. The government also mobilized business and society to cooperate with the government's efforts against Falun Gong. Families and workplaces were urged to report the practitioners and their activities. Many Falun Gong practitioners fled the country. They continue to practice the Falun Gong overseas while protesting the government's brutal suppression of their members in China.

TIBETAN BUDDHISTS AND XINJIANG MUSLIMS

The Chinese government continues to exercise political control over Buddhist activities in Tibet, including the restriction of religious

Falun Gong practitioners meditate next to a poster calling on Chinese president Jiang Zemin to stop what they say is the killing of the sect members, during a protest in a Hong Kong park Wednesday, June 19, 2002. The protesters also demanded an explanation from the Hong Kong government for allegedly barring about 120 Falun Gong practitioners from visiting Hong Kong to demonstrate during the handover anniversary. The Chinese characters read: "Help Persecuted Falun Gong Members in Mainland China" and "Jiang's Latest Crazy Order: Kill Everybody." (AP Photo/Anat Givon.)

study before age 18, the expulsion of unapproved monks from monasteries, the implementation of quotas on the number of monks in an attempt to reduce the spiritual population, and the forced recitation of patriotic scripts in support of the Chinese government. Beijing coerces denunciations of the Dalai Lama as a spiritual leader, human rights fighter, and peace envoy. The Dalai Lama is described as an ex-leader of Tibetan Buddhism under the wing of the anti-China forces in the West, and his government in exile is condemned as illegal since it has betrayed China and the Tibetan people.

The Chinese government has accused the Dalai Lama of being the linchpin of alleged plots to separate Tibet from China.[12] In June 2003, Chinese authorities arrested three Tibetans in the region's capital, Lhasa, for alleged separatist activities. One of them was a Lhasa City CPPCC member, and the other two were junior students at Tibet University. They were accused of involvement in "activities to split the motherland." Many believe the arrests came amid tighter restrictions on civil liberties put in place leading up to the Dalai Lama's birthday, as happens every year. A 2003 circular warned residents against burning incense, hanging prayer flags, or visiting temples or monasteries. In early 2007, seven Tibetan teenagers (ages between 14 and 16) were arrested because they wrote "antigovernmental" slogans on the walls of a village police station. Their slogans included calling for the return of the Dalai Lama and a free Tibet. The government views Tibetan Buddhism as complicit in these efforts.[13]

In Tibet, authorities continue to control Buddhist activities in an effort to quash alleged "separatism." The repression of religious freedom remains commonplace in the Tibetan Autonomous Region (TAR). Many Tibetan Buddhists have been arrested, detained without public trial, and tortured for expressing their views or organizing activities without government permission. On September 30, 2006, Chinese border patrol troops opened fire on 70 Tibetans who tried to cross the border into Nepal; a 17-year-old Buddhist nun, Kelsang Nmtso, died, and several others were wounded.

In March 2008, a large-scale Buddhist demonstration began in Tibet and several surrounding provinces on the forty-ninth anniversary of the 1959 uprising in Tibet against the central government. On March 14, the protest in Lhasa turned violent between Tibetans and non-Tibetan groups and between protesters and police; these clashes became known as the "3/14 Riots." By March 17, the TAR governor announced that 16 people had been confirmed dead and 200 were injured from the violence. On March 28, the government confirmed that 28 civilians and 1 police officer were dead; 325 civilians were injured, 58 of them critically, along with 241 police officers. According to the India-based Tibetan government in exile, more than 220 Tibetans were killed in the crackdown after March 14, and the Chinese government arrested at least 7,000 Tibetans from various parts of Tibet.

The riots spread outside of the TAR for the first time. More than 5,000 demonstrators, mostly ethnic Tibetans and Buddhist monks, marched down the streets in Gansu province on March 15. Police used tear gas and force to break up the demonstrations. By

March 18, according to the Tibetan government in exile, 19 Tibetan demonstrators were shot dead by police. Demonstrations also took place in the northwestern province of Qinghai and western province of Sichuan. On March 16, Tibetan monks and police clashed in Ngawa county, Sichuan, and there are claims that police shot between 13 and 20 protesters and at least one policeman was killed.

The 3/14 Riots and the crackdown in Tibet shocked the international community, including athletes who were ready to come to Beijing for the 2008 Olympic Games in August. Some Western countries and international organizations called for a boycott of the event, but others opposed the idea. The Dalai Lama reiterated that he was against any boycott because Chinese people should not be blamed for the situation in his homeland. The Olympic torch was lit in Greece on March 24, 2008, but the torch relay faced Tibet protestors throughout its journey across the globe.

On April 29, 2008, the Lhasa Intermediate Court sentenced 30 Tibetans to three years to life in prison for their participations in the 3/14 Riots. In 2009, the Chinese government executed four Tibetans in connection with their involvement with the riots. On December 28, 2009, authorities in the northwestern province of Qinghai sentenced Dhondup Wangchen, a Tibetan filmmaker, to six years in prison; the director and producer of a documentary about the 3/14 Riots, Leaving Fear Behind, he was charged with "splitting the motherland."

The Xinjiang Uyghur Autonomous Region (XUAR) is the only province in the country where the ethnic population outnumbers the Han Chinese. This northwestern region comprises more than 8 million Uyghurs and 2.5 million other ethnic minorities. The Han Chinese population is 6.4 million, up from 300,000 in 1949. Most Uyghurs are poor farmers, and at least 25 percent are illiterate. The XUAR government maintains control over the religious and political expression of the Muslim population. The government allows religious activities only in state-controlled churches, temples, and mosques. All religious programs and cleric appointments have to get the governmental approval. No youth programs are permitted in the churches, temples, and mosques, and minors are not allowed to participate in worship activities.[14] These restrictions have alienated the Turkic-speaking Uyghur population in Xinjiang, and people are concerned that the harsh policies may fuel separatist fervor.

A Chinese security guard, right, attempts to stop Australian Liam Phelan, left, and American Han Shan of New York from holding up a banner that reads "No Olympics for China until Tibet Is Free" and Olympic rings shaped like barbed wire from a Chinese style bridge at the Ethnic Minorities Park in Beijing, 2004. The two were representing the International Tibet Support Network, a body of Tibet related non-government organizations with a political mandate aimed at ending human rights violations in Tibet. Beijing's Olympics in 2008 became a target for many interest groups seeking their voices to be heard. The two were later detained by Chinese police. (AP Photo/Ng Han Guan.)

In November 2004, top Chinese officials in the XUAR government called for an intensification of "ideological work" among the ethnic Uyghur university students. Local officials were also ordered to report anyone fasting during the month of Ramadan. According to the Five Pillars of Islam, there are five practices every Muslim must follow: witness, pray, give alms, fast during the month of Ramadan, and make a pilgrimage to Mecca, the city of the prophet, where certain rituals must be completed by the believer at specific times. According to the Islamic tradition, during Ramadan, no food or drink is allowed for the adult population during the daytime; restaurants remain closed from dawn to dusk in most Islamic countries. But the XUAR government ignores the Islamic tradition. City officials ensure that restaurants stay open during Ramadan, and college administrators must report anyone who fasts. In many grade schools, before the children leave school, they receive free candy to eat. Xinjiang authorities collected the passports of Muslims in June 2007 during the traditional period for a pilgrimage to visit Mecca, as the government tried to prevent any non-state-approved pilgrimage. The XUAR government also indoctrinates clerics, civil servants, and teachers against the "three evil forces"—separatism, religious extremism, and terrorism.

Authorities have used the international war on terror as a pretext for harshly cracking down on independent Muslim religious groups. The government, for instance, considers some Islamic Turks to be separatists and terrorists and has stated that an "East Turkistan" movement has used the banner of "human rights," "freedom of religion," and "interests of ethnic minorities" to further its cause. The movement aims to achieve an independent Uyghur republic of East Turkistan. Even though some independent analysts question the existence of such a group, the government believes that the Islamic Turks are calling for separation and independence.

After the September 11, 2001, attacks on the United States, the Chinese government intensified its efforts. The government has stated that the East Turkistan supporters claim "the Chinese government is using every opportunity to oppress ethnic minorities," and that the East Turkistan groups support terrorism. Thus, authorities have a "Strike Hard" policy meant to crush Islamic activities seen as supportive of the East Turkistan movement. In January 2007, the XUAR government sent armed police to raid a village, during which 18 people were killed and 17 arrested. The government described the village as a "terrorist training camp" of the East Turkistan Islamic Movement. In November, under terrorism charges, 5 of the 17 were sentenced to death and one to life imprisonment.

Authorities also target some Muslim individuals, such as exiled activist Rebiya Kadeer. She was a successful businesswoman in Xinjiang with the local nickname "the Millionaire," became a member of the CPPCC, and held a position at the United Nations' Fourth World Conference on Women, held in Beijing in 1995. Kadeer, however, was barred from reelection in 1998 because she refused to condemn her husband, Sidik Rouzi, who lives in the United States and actively participates in protesting the Chinese government's policies toward the

Uyghurs. In 1999, Kadeer was arrested and thrown in jail for sending newspaper articles to her husband—which was seen as leaking state secrets. In 2004, during her imprisonment, she won the Rafto Prize for human rights.

The U.S. government pressed for her release, and in March 2005, the Chinese government released her to U.S. custody. In 2006, she was nominated for the Nobel Peace Prize, while the Chinese government labeled her a terrorist. Kadeer became the leader of the Uyghur American Association in 2007. In April 2007, her son, Ablikim Abdiriyim, was sentenced to nine years' imprisonment for "having spread secessionist articles over the Internet." In the same month, another political prisoner, Huseyincan Celil, was sentenced to life imprisonment. Celil, who had been arrested earlier, had fled China in 2000. Uzbek authorities forcibly returned him in 2006, after he had become a Canadian citizen. The Chinese government ignored his Canadian citizenship, and Canadian diplomats were not allowed to attend his trial.

After bloody riots in Xinjiang on July 5, 2009, the government blamed the demonstrations and violence on overseas separatist organizations such as the Uyghur American Association and the World Uyghur Congress, which protested China's religious and ethnic policies against the Uyghurs in Xinjiang. On July 18, a Chinese official reported 197 dead and 1,721 injured, although the World Uyghur Congress has reported a much higher tally, at around 600 dead. The official also confirmed at that time that more than 1,500 suspected rioters had been arrested in Urumqi and other parts of Xinjiang. The government condemned the riots as "premeditated and planned." One of the XUAR officials, Eligen Imibakhi, chair of the Standing Committee of the Xinjiang Regional People's Congress, blamed the "7/5 Riots" on "extremism, separatism, and terrorism."[15] The Chinese government continued its suppression on these "three forces" within Uyghur and Muslim movements. By December 2009, authorities had sentenced 22 Uyghurs to death for their participation in the July 5 ethnic rioting.

As long as the government maintains the dual policy, the Chinese people's struggle for religious freedom will continue into the second decade of the twenty-first century. After 30 years of economic reform and opening up to the outside world, many Chinese have improved their standard of living and moved into the middle class. However, a large number of less fortunate individuals, particularly the less well educated, unemployed, urban poor, and much of the rural population, have experienced great injustice as the gap between the rich and the poor continues to grow. Many are looking for answers not from the government but from the spiritual world. This is a time when they truly need new guidance and must continue their search for belief.

The government faces a difficult dilemma. It can either provide new opportunities to decrease economic problems or allow more freedom of religious belief. There is another way for authorities to ease the tension and maintain a harmony between the government and the religious groups. Freedom House, an international human rights organization, has suggested that the Chinese government should open channels such as town meetings and public hearings that allow Catholics, Protestants, Buddhists, Muslims, and other believers to express their concerns and provide suggestions. Some of the officials of the state who have violated constitutional rights and civil liberties of the citizens should be punished by the government.[16]

Chapter 4

New Technology, New Battlefields

Because of the revolutionary changes from paper communication to digital technology, few areas of research in contemporary China pose more difficulties than the study of the mass media. According to the official statistics, by the end of 2003, 30.1 million computers in the country were connected to the Internet, and the number of households that logged on reached 79.5 million, the second highest in the world.[1] That year, the number of households with telephones increased to 263.3 million, and mobile phone users increased by 62.7 million, to 268.7 million. With 532 million telephone users, or 42 of every 100 individuals, China is one of the leading countries in terms of communications development. In 2005, the "Super Girl" contest, a television program broadcast by satellite out of Hunan province along the same format as *American Idol*, used votes by millions of cellular phone users to determine the winner. These tremendous changes in communications technology, particularly the transition from printed media to more rapid, digital formats, are challenging the authority of official Chinese political and social institutions.

The digital revolution has had a strong and positive impact in the public arena and civil society. As the Chinese people become better informed and connected, both the impact of the digital transformation on the evolution of democratic and civil rights as well as the influence it will have on the flexibility of government policy in the context of this major social and political transition are uncertain. In the past, the Chinese Communist Party had used the media as a means to articulate and build support for its policies. In recent years, however, the Party Center has adjusted its approach, while still maintaining its control of the mass media and public opinion. This chapter examines government

A Chinese sales attendant stands behind cell phone promotional ads at a shopping mall in Jinan, 2004. Cell phone sales continue to rise in one of the largest markets for telecommunications as Chinese seek to buy the latest and most expensive sets to look fashionable. (AP Photo/Ng Han Guan.)

policies concerning this issue. The stories of Chinese journalists and foreign reporters in the country will provide unique insights into those who shaped the struggle for the freedom of information and press during the first decade of the twenty-first century. Furthermore, the chapter places individuals participating in the struggle for personal rights in the context of international events and the greater Chinese society.

PUBLIC INFORMATION AND OFFICIAL REGULATIONS

In the 1950s through the 1970s, the Party Center began using domestic media outlets as a mouthpiece for its propaganda machine, both to mobilize the masses and to manage the impressions it gave of the country to its own citizens and the outside world. During the economic reform and liberalization movements of the 1980s, the government began to adopt more flexible policies toward the media with an emphasis on rights guaranteed by the constitution. Article 35 of the 1982 Constitution promised: "Citizens of the People's Republic of China enjoy freedom of speech, of the press, of assembly, of association, of procession and of demonstration."

Later, at all levels, the government established the spokesperson system, beginning in the Ministry of Foreign Affairs in 1983, opening an important information channel only for diplomatic and other important political occasions. In 1999, China implemented a spokesperson system in the provincial governments, with the provincial government of Guangdong in south China as the first. The city government of Shanghai introduced spokespersons in its 24 departments in April 2002.[2] After the outbreak of Severe Acute Respiratory Syndrome (SARS) in the fall of 2002, the Chinese government tried to improve its image by upgrading its spokesperson system. In early 2003, for example, Beijing began a training program for spokespersons; by September, the training program had involved a hundred representatives from 66 central government ministries and departments. In early 2006, the Ministry of Justice began to install a spokesperson system for the courts at the provincial, county, and city levels. The system, which provides a new channel for public information and communication, has improved the image of the government and judicial system.

The authorities have stated that they have made new efforts to increase the transparency of administrative affairs. The National People's Congress and its Standing Committee have engaged more and more in shaping the major policies and exercising the legislative power of the state. The NPC has also begun to pay attention to petitions from ordinary people. In 2003, for example, the NPC Standing Committee received 31,000 visits to its Beijing offices and handled more than 57,000 letters from all over the country. In the meantime, the Chinese People's Political Consultative Conference has also actively participated in the policy debates and social survey in order to play a better supervisory role in the government. In 2003, the CPPCC National Committee investigated specific issues, such as rural poverty, which resulted in 37 investigative reports and 114 proposals within specialized fields. The other parties under the CPPCC submitted 84 proposals and passed on 1,674 reports of public opinion through the CPPCC.[3]

Although the public's access to information has improved, the Party Center continues to exercise strict control over the media, effectively keeping the bulk of China's press as components of a vast national propaganda system. With some slow changes, the government maintains control of news outlets in several different ways.

The first means of control is through government regulation. Even though Article 35 of the Constitution guarantees freedom of the press, Article 51 makes it clear that this liberty cannot infringe on the "interests of the state." A series of national agencies such as the Propaganda Department of the CCP Central Committee, the Ministry of Public Security, the General Administration for Press and Publications (GAPP) of the State Council, and the Ministry of the Information Industry establish regulations and rules for the prohibition of any material that "harms the honor or the interests of the nation," "spreads rumors," or "harms the credibility of a government agency."[4] These vague guidelines and amorphous legislative acts are an impediment to the freedom of the media.

Aside from establishing rules for the publication of books, the GAPP regulates more than 9,000 weekly and monthly magazines and journals throughout the country. It issues regulations on a regular basis in an attempt to control news, public opinion, and editorials. Each magazine or journal must follow strict directions from the relevant government departments or risk losing its publishing license. The Propaganda Department of the CCP Central Committee also played an important role in controlling publications and domestic media. In August 2008, for example, the Chinese government allowed foreign and domestic journalists to interview citizens and report during the Beijing Olympic Games, but the Propaganda Department set up many rules for the Chinese reporters. According to the department's directives, the domestic media were barred from reporting on the Tibetan and Uyghur movements, news from foreign websites, and problems in the Olympic security system, among other topics.

Local governments at the provincial, county, and city levels also set up their own guidelines for the restriction of media activities. For example, in December 2001, the Dunhuang city government in northwestern Gansu province issued its "Opinion on Strengthening

the Supervision of Correspondents' Offices in Dunhuang and Journalists Conducting Interviews in Dunhuang." The city government's
"opinion" specifically stipulates:

> Critical reports that involve the leadership of this municipality
> and cadres ranked assistant section chief and above must be
> submitted to the local propaganda department [of the party
> committee] for approval, and must also be transmitted to the
> persons concerned and the relevant leaders.[5]

According to a report by an international human rights organization, in August 2002, all news media in the city of Lanzhou, also in
Gansu province, received an official letter from the Public Security Bureau of Lanzhou. The city put 16 journalists on a blacklist because
they had published "inaccurate" reports about city police officers. The
journalists on this blacklist were "banned from future interviews and
investigations with police and public security officers."[6]

The second measure of state control is government ownership of all
media, in whole or in part. This concentrated control protects the party
authorities, provides political supervision, and ensures that the companies are run by handpicked executives and staff. All reporters, editors,
producers, and administrators are employed by either the central or
local government and are closely monitored. However, the newly developed market economy has put more and more pressure on the Chinese
media to consider the revenues provided by advertisements, subscribers,
and the viewership. The bureaucratic nature of the Chinese media has
begun to give in to these economic pressures and embrace commerciali-
zation and business strategies. The government has shifted its control
mechanisms to include elaborate censorship and licensing procedures.
Increasingly, journalists can enjoy relatively broad discretion in their
ability to report on topics such as sports, entertainment, consumer life-
styles, and local news without extensive political implications.

The third method of media control is government censorship of sensitive stories from the bottom up, focusing on the news reporting system.
Each reporter must know the line between what is permitted and what is
forbidden. They are expected to practice self-censorship, since their jobs
are on the line. Then their editors use the same criteria to approve or dis-
approve the news report. They can reject an article or reassign a reporter

with the use of often overt intimidation. Producers and directors act as further instruments of control. If a reporter or editor is perceived to have crossed the line, his or her employer can kill the product and relocate, demote, or even fire the individuals responsible as punishment. On important issues, the upper management must report to party officials and the chief executive officers of their outlet for final approval. These latter two groups of officials receive the party's instructions, reporting guidelines, and official news releases on a daily basis from the central government's agencies, including the CCP Central Committee's Propaganda Department and the official Xinhua (New China) News Agency, or from local organizations such as city and provincial party committees. In the occasional instance when a newspaper or television station makes a mistake by releasing a piece that differs from the official party line, the outlet's leadership either lost their jobs or faced criminal charges.

The fourth measure of control is the government's control of access to information. Many sites and records, such as courthouses, police stations, and city and provincial government offices, remain closed to reporters. The government controls all information concerning the Tibetan areas, for instance, as well as access to the region. This makes it difficult to accurately determine the scope and condition of civil liberties there. In many cases, reporters must have permission before they begin interviews or investigations. It is even more difficult for foreign reporters to gain these types of access. A major exception was made before and during the 2008 Olympic Games in Beijing, when the Chinese government issued regulations that, from January 1, 2007, to October 17, 2008, gave foreign correspondents permission to interview anyone who consented. Bao Tong, a well-known dissident who has been under house arrest at his Beijing home since the 1989 student-led prodemocracy movement in Tiananmen Square, said he was very pleased with these new rules.

This temporary reprieve from censorship did not, however, include Chinese reporters or the Chinese assistants who worked for foreign correspondents. The government and pro-party media continue to crack down on "unofficial news"—officially called "fake news" and "illegal news coverage." Some Chinese journalists and writers continue to be harassed, detained, and intimidated by police officers or local thugs if they fail to follow official regulations. Bao Tong and other dissidents also questioned the durability of the new interview policy beyond the Olympic Games, warning that nothing could be taken for granted. "We should be vigilant," Bao said, "because there are still plenty of evil forces in China that would

A Chinese police officer questions a journalist about a handout from the Reporters Without Borders depicting the Olympic rings made from handcuffs in Beijing, 2007. Police roughed up journalists at a rare protest in Beijing, staged by the free-press advocacy group that accused the government of failing to meet promises for greater media freedom one year before the 2008 Olympic Games. (AP Photo/Ng Han Guan.)

love to rip apart press freedom."[7] During an interview in February 2008, he cited the case of a reporter from the *China Trade Journal* who was beaten to death after trying to get to the truth behind a mining disaster in central Shanxi province.

"GOOD NEWS" AND "BAD REPORTERS"

State control of the news is successful because the government manages all media outlets, with powers that include the hiring of journalists, production, and the restriction of access to information. Newspapers, radio, television stations, and journal publishers received "reporting guidelines" from the Central Propaganda Department of the CCP on a regular basis. The department provides a list of the topics that should not be reported, including some sensitive topics or negative images of the government.

It is tough to be a journalist in China, since one may have to play the role of "party mouthpiece" while trying to tell the true story. Those with a sense of social responsibility must balance their reports by reinforcing a positive image of the state and deemphasizing the object of their report, such as corruption, by stating that it occurs strictly at lower levels, or that accidents resulting in the loss of life resulted strictly from the individual actions of a minority of officials. On the one hand, these self-protective approaches at least guarantee the journalists' personal safety, job security, and professional career. On the other hand, because all that people are allowed to watch, read, and listen to are official reports, it is easy for the government to cover up major issues such as mining disasters, mass poisonings, and labor uprisings.

The SARS outbreak in southern China in 2002–2003 is a major example of the government controlling access to information. In its primary viral form, this disease has a 70 percent mortality rate. It began in southern Guangdong province in November 2002. While the government tried to take some measures to control the epidemic, it did not allow the media to report the outbreak in south China. The government did not inform the World Health Organization (WHO) of the SARS outbreak until February 2003. During these critical months, the government restricted media coverage and did not allow reporters to interview concerned families and medical personnel. Chinese authorities attempted to preserve public confidence and assure foreign investors and tourists that everything was business as usual.

In early April, Chinese health officials insisted that the epidemic was under "effective control." In Beijing, they reported only thirty-seven cases and continued to delay reporting or give false figures. In May, Chinese censors blocked the airing of an American-based CNN (Cable News Network) program that criticized Beijing's handling of the SARS epidemic. This lack of openness resulted in delayed efforts to control the disease, and the censorship process predated the worst of the outbreak. By July 31, there were 5,328 cases in the country and

349 fatalities. In the interim, the disease spread from China and rapidly infected individuals in approximately 37 countries around the world. Following this rapid spread of the disease, the government acknowledged it had underreported the number of SARS cases, and, as a result, both the mayor of Beijing and the health minister were fired, but only after the outbreak had killed more than 700 people in nine countries.

Frequent cover-ups and a general lack of openness on the part of the government indicate that Chinese authorities do not yet fully respect the freedom of the press. Throughout 2005 and 2006, critical media reports on corruption in the appropriation of land and environmental damage were followed by intensified crackdowns on journalists, including several incidents that resulted in the dismissal of chief editors, the closure of popular newspapers, and violent attacks on journalists attempting to cover sensitive stories. The government-instituted control of information is a crucial barrier to the formation of an independent civil society. Attacks on the independence of the press have a ripple effect on society, and crackdowns on this sector discourage others, such as grassroots activists, petitioners, and dissatisfied workers, from speaking out.

Chinese journalists continue to risk severe repercussions if they report on and publish controversial views to the domestic population or forward them to overseas audiences. In the spring of 2001, hundreds of residents of Shangzhou, Shaanxi province, were found to be infected with AIDS, a rate of 4 percent, which far exceeds that of some African countries. Several journalists for *Shaanxi Ribao* (Shaanxi Daily) provided the public with a true picture of the AIDS situation and reported that the spread of the virus was caused by the selling of blood in Henan province. Later, these journalists were investigated and prosecuted for "violating the State Secrets Law concerning unauthorized publication of information on serious epidemics."[8]

In 2005, Chinese authorities had 32 journalists imprisoned, which is higher than in any other country. In 2007, 29 were imprisoned. From 2000 to 2009, for nine consecutive years, China has been one of the leading nations in the incarceration of journalists. According to the Committee to Protect Journalists, some of those prosecuted have served long sentences. Two, Chen Renjie and Lin Youping, have been in jail since 1983 for publishing a pamphlet entitled "Ziyou Bao" (Freedom Report), and reporter Chen Biling was executed.[9]

The international rights organization Freedom House described the case of Shi Tao, a similar criminal prosecution and punishment by the government against an individual writer. In 2004, Shi, an editor with the *Dangdai Shangbao* (Contemporary Business News) in Changsha, in southern Hunan province, was arrested for "leaking state secrets." His actual offense was divulging the Propaganda Department's instructions to his newspaper. In April 2005, Shi was given 10 years in prison by the Changsha Intermediate People's Court.

In another example, in February 2006, editors of *Bingdian* (Freezing Point), a popular weekly magazine, were removed after an article criticized China's textbooks.[10] Human rights groups also followed the death of Lan Chengzhang closely. Lan was a reporter with *China Trade News* and was investigating an illegal coal mine in Datong, Shanxi province. Lan was murdered in January 2007 during his investigation at Datong.

In mid-August 2007, the country was shocked by the news that the recently completed Fenghuang Bridge had collapsed in Hunan province, killing 64 people. Several reporters conducted an investigation that led to a corruption case. During their interviews, however, a group of unidentified thugs interrupted the proceedings and began kicking and punching the five journalists who were interviewing witnesses to the bridge collapse. When the police arrived on the scene, they arrested the journalists, not the assailants. Law enforcement, criminal prosecution, and punishments have been employed by the government against domestic journalists, writers, and their controversial writings.[11]

Many magazines and journalists face the threat of closure from government departments if they expose official corruption or political problems. To survive, some of them must change their tone or give up on what they intended to publish. *Baixing* (Commoners) became a popular monthly when it ran hard-hitting exposés of governmental corruption and the abuse of power among local officials in the countryside. In August 2006, for example, it printed an article entitled "Ground-level Investigation into Evictions and Demolitions in Jiangyin City" on a local official scandal. The article explored how the city officials had taken land from local families and evicted them. The municipal police were also involved and had imprisoned the rural families' representatives in manacles. In late 2006, the *Baixing* editor-in-chief came under pressure from various government agencies, and by early 2007, he and nearly all of his team, from deputy editors and reporters to circulation and advertising staff, had to leave the magazine. In May 2007, *Baixing* had a complete makeover, in which it changed from a cutting-edge magazine into a cultural and lifestyle digest of previously published materials. The magazine no longer employed its own in-house staff writers or published original articles. The government, including the GAPP and the Ministry of Agriculture, in this case, effectively neutralized a popular periodical.

Another successful magazine, *Sanlian Shenghuo Zhoukan* (Sanlian Life Weekly), reported on the Tangshan earthquake, a major natural disaster in 1976 still on the list of politically sensitive topics. After publishing the article, the magazine was ordered, on threat of closure, to stay away from these types of topics. This order came from the Propaganda Department of the Party's Central Committee, which tightly controls China's media. Later the executive editor of the magazine was demoted in connection with the publication of the articles.

As noted earlier, the Chinese government limits foreign reporters' and journalists' access to information. Beijing continues to jam radio broadcasts of Radio Free Asia (RFA), the British Broadcasting Corporation (BBC), and the Voice of America (VOA). Broadcasting to China in Chinese, Tibetan, and Uyghur languages, these services nevertheless have a large audience that includes activists, ordinary citizens, and even government officials. Some of these institutions' reporters, researchers, and assistants are not allowed to conduct interviews, visit sites, or take pictures. In September 2004, Zhao Yan, a researcher for the *New York Times*, was detained for "providing state secrets to foreigners." Zhao had revealed the retirement of Jiang Zemin before the official announcements. He was subsequently charged with fraud and sentenced to three years' imprisonment in a trial closed to the public. In March 2007, residents of Yongzhou, Hunan province, went to the streets in protest of a large increase in the public bus fare. Some of the protesters turned violent and set some buses on fire. When BBC reporters went to the scene, they were stopped by armed police.

In September 2007, two reporters from Britain's Channel Four, Andrew Carter and Aidan Hartey, interviewed and filmed visitors appealing to the central government for assistance. Beijing's police arrested the journalists and destroyed their films. During their interrogations, the police demanded the reporters sign a confession that they had violated the Chinese law. The Foreign Correspondent's Club of China (FCCC) reported in September 2008 that after the central government had issued its temporary regulations giving foreign correspondents permission to interview people freely in advance of the Beijing Olympics, local authorities continued to interrupt the travel and interviews of foreign journalists and that incidents of harassment rose sharply.

On January 24–26, 2008, for example, a German television crew traveled to eastern Shandong province to interview Yuan Weijing, wife of imprisoned human rights activist Chen Guangcheng. When the German reporters entered her neighborhood, a group of thugs began to attack the crew, throwing rocks and pushing them away from Yuan's house.

The FCCC reported 30 cases of "reporting interference" in the month before and during the Olympic Games. On July 22, several Beijing residents got injured when a huge crowd attempted to purchase Olympics tickets and police lost control. When a group of Hong Kong reporters tried to cover these events by taking pictures and interviewing the people at the scene, Beijing police manhandled the reporters. In another incident, on August 4, four days before the Opening Ceremonies of the Beijing Olympic Games, a bomb exploded and killed eight People's Armed Police policemen in Kashgar, Xinjiang. Two Japanese journalists who arrived in Kashgar and tried to cover the aftermath of the deadly attack were arrested by local police. They were detained for days and beaten by the Xinjiang police several times. And on August 13, a journalist for ITN (Independent Television News) attempted to cover a protest relating to Tibet near the Olympic village. Beijing police pushed him away and detained him.[12]

According to the FCCC, between January 1 and December 2, 2008, there were 178 incidents of harassment of foreign journalists when they conducted interviews, up from 160 cases for all of 2007. Recently, representatives from World Press Freedom met with Chinese officials and requested to visit the reporters. Even though the Chinese officials agreed to the request, a visit has not been arranged. In its annual report on world media freedom, the American-based Freedom House rated China at the same level as Iran, with only Communist countries and dictatorships, such as Cuba, North Korea, and Myanmar (Burma), having poorer records of freedom of the press. World Press Freedom ranked China 163rd on its annual report on global freedom of the press.

INTERNET POLICING AND NEW BATTLES

In China, the Internet has become a popular medium for communication, education, and business operations. According to official statistics, the country had a total of 103 million users as of June 30, 2005, with particularly high numbers among youths between the ages of 18 and 24. That number had grown to an estimated 144 million users at the end of 2006 and 298 million in 2008. According to research completed by Tsinghua University (one of China's top technology universities), the country had 100 million bloggers in 2007. Among Internet users, 91 percent reportedly have broadband access.

While encouraging Internet use for business and educational purposes, the government has kept tight controls on its use for political discussion. The authorities worry about the possibility of online anti-government activities organized by dissent "netizens," who might mobilize opposition from the country's fast-growing population of cyber-surfers. The Party Center has strengthened its control over the Internet within China by setting up new regulations and establishing a new central governmental agency. At a Politburo meeting in January 2007, President Hu Jintao said that the Internet was related to the country's safety and security and was a source of sensitive information. As a result, the State Council established the Bureau of Internet in the State Council's Media Department, while a mirror organization, the Bureau of Internet Propaganda, was formed in the Office of External Propaganda in the CCP Central Committee.

Government censorship and surveillance have increased in cyberspace in response to the Internet's growing popularity and its use as a medium for activism throughout China. More than a dozen regulations relating to the Internet have been implemented by the Party Central Committee's Department of Propaganda, the Ministry of Public Security, the Ministry of the Information Industry, the Ministry of Culture, and relevant departments of the ministries at various levels. In May 2007, for example, China's Internet authorities issued the new rules entitled "Regulations for the Management of Internet Publishing." These new guidelines brought online magazines, or webzines, under the same controls as print publications. Webzines must now obtain prior agreement from the GAPP before seeking approval from the Ministry of the Information Industry to set up a telecommunications business.

In September, the Ministry of the Information Industry issued a new set of rules aimed at curbing the spread of "interactive" Internet sites such as bulletin boards, chat rooms, blogs, and discussion forums. According to these guidelines, all providers offering these services must reapply for a license and, if their applications are denied, are to be closed down. The Ministry of Public Security and local police forces have trained a large number of police to monitor the Internet around the clock. The central and local governments have heavily invested in new technology to upgrade their monitoring of Web content. By August 2005, the government had already spent at least $800 million on state-of-the-art equipment to control its citizens online.

Western pundits have dubbed China's elaborate system of censorship "the Great Firewall of China." American and other foreign information technology companies' contributions to official censorship raise serious issues concerning socially responsible corporate practices and policies.

New advances in technology have greatly enabled the Chinese government, through several different measures, to tighten its grip on cyberspace. The first of these is instant control over the content of online information exchanges. Officials have developed lists of sensitive keywords, or "bad words," that are used to facilitate censorship. Major search engines, service providers, and technology companies—including the U.S.-based Yahoo, Cisco, and Microsoft—have been cooperating with the Chinese government to restrict information that includes terms such as "1989 Tiananmen Incident," "Taiwan independence," or "democracy" or that mentions the outlawed Falun Gong "evil cult" or "separatist" elements in Tibet and Xinjiang. Whenever these topics occur in search engine results, whatever content the government does not like that originates in China is blocked by servers. The government also censors pornography and online religious materials. This instantaneous "bad word" system of control is expected to increase self-censorship by netizens who realize the problem and will then stop writing about these sensitive topics.

A second measure used to control Internet communication is enhanced identification procedures, including online registration, identifying users by their real name, and password verification. These measures are performed by public security departments, police, or Internet service providers acting on behalf of the authorities. Chinese bloggers who use their own domain name are required to register, a process that requires providing the names and addresses of all site administrators, who are in turn responsible for moderating site content. Thus, organizers must scrutinize their own and others' speech for fear of getting into trouble themselves. Residents in Shenzhen, Guangdong province, for example, are required to have their real identities verified by a company in Shenzhen if they wish to use its instant messaging software to engage in group discussions. Through this procedure, a person's actual identity is connected with the opinion expressed online, providing the authorities with more control in cyberspace and greater surveillance capabilities of public opinion. Because of the loss of privacy, however, many users are not comfortable with the real-name registration.

The third measure the government uses to exercise control over the Internet is to have its own bloggers and commentators. The Propaganda Department and public security departments have trained a network of online commentators to manipulate the opinions expressed in Internet forums and message groups. They either are employees of the government or are paid by the departments as a part-time job. They hide their real identities to facilitate introducing government ideas or fabricating false public opinion through Web pages, blogs, online discussion forums, university bulletin board systems, and e-mail messages. Even though the government has these multiple control mechanisms, it can always shut down websites or individual blogs if officials think it necessary.

The well-developed government network is in fact supported by the corporate and private sectors in the information technology world. In the spring of 2005, Yahoo-China merged with Chinese-owned Alibaba. After this $1 billion merger, Yahoo, as an international partner and 40 percent stakeholder, had to follow Beijing on the issues of censorship and devolve all related decisions to the local management teams.

In 2006, Google cooperated with China by fracturing the Internet and creating "Google.cn." This local Chinese-language search engine soon became very popular, but it is run within Chinese censorship laws. Chinese authorities used the website to spy on Chinese political dissidents by reading their e-mails and checking on their search results.

In January 2010, Google announced that the company would no longer cooperate with China's censorship laws and would stop censoring

In this January 15, 2010, photo, a Chinese Google user presents flowers in front of a Google sign outside Google China's headquarters in Beijing. Google's accusation that its e-mail accounts were hacked from China landed like a bombshell because it cast light on a problem few companies will discuss: the pervasive threat from China-based cyber attacks. (AP Photo/Vincent Thian, File.)

Google.cn, even if the Internet giant would have to pull out of China. The company said that it was prepared to shut down its local Chinese-language search engine, unless "it is allowed to run it uncensored."[13] Before the talks began between Google and Chinese authorities, different responses to Google's decision had come from all directions. International rights organizations praised Google's stance against China's violation of human and civil rights.

It is significant for Google to set up a new principled stand on free speech and human rights. It is also important for Google to publicly challenge China's censorship, since the Chinese government has recently claimed that constraints on free speech in the Internet are crucial to political stability and economic prosperity.

ONLINE GUERRILLAS AND CYBER WARFARE

The Chinese government shuts down websites with "unauthorized" content that includes politically sensitive information or antigovernment material. From July to August 2007, authorities closed several dozen websites, including Briefing China's Development and the Forum for Contemporary Poems because of "violations of the government regulations." Under such pressure, foreign Internet servers on the government list of the "bad websites," for example, the American-based Godaddy.com, have had to stop service to their Chinese customers who registered and paid for access. In August 2007, Shanghai Internet police shut down the online journal *Minjiang* (Min River) and even blocked its overseas edition, hosted on a non-Chinese server. Also in 2007, officials reported that the government had shut down tens of thousands of websites as part of a nationwide crackdown on "illegal websites."

The same year, the Chinese government also shut down a site dedicated to those with hepatitis-B, Hbvhbv.com, which had been running for six years without any interference. China now has 120 million known carriers of the disease, and this site had been a strong force in fighting social discrimination against those infected. The HBV forums had provided a slender lifeline to those affected by the virus and who were experiencing severe difficulties as a result of their diagnosis.

After the 7/5 Riots in Xinjiang, the Chinese government cut off almost all Internet access to the entire region of 19 million people from July 2009 to February 2010. The online blackout was lifted temporarily before the Chinese New Year.

Writers, bloggers, and journalists often face punishments that range from immediate dismissal from their positions and jobs to prosecution and jail terms for such offenses as sending news via e-mail to those outside of the country or posting articles critical of the political system. Authorities enforce official regulations and punish those who violate them, especially political dissidents. In May 2004, Du Daobin, a former government official in Hubei province, was arrested and charged with "inciting subversion of the state's power" after he posted several essays online that were critical of government policy. By the time of his arrest, officials had detained more than 30 individuals as part of a crackdown on online dissent. As mentioned earlier, Shi Tao, the editor arrested for divulging the CCP Propaganda Department's instructions to his paper, was sentenced in April 2005 to 10 years imprisonment for sending an e-mail to an overseas rights group detailing the activities of the same CCP Central Committee organization.

Online author Li Hong (the pen name of Zhang Jianhong) was one of those punished for expressing her political opinions on the

Internet. Li created a website, Aegean Sea, that published news, articles, and comments. Some of her discussions were critical of government policies, and she became considered an online political dissident. Before the end of 2006, Li was arrested, and in March 2007, she was sentenced to six years' imprisonment under the charge of "inciting subversion of the government." That summer, after she began to serve her prison term, she became very sick but was denied a medical parole.

In November 2008, authorities in the eastern province of Jiangsu arrested a prominent blogger, Guo Quan. Guo was a founding member of the prodemocracy Chinese New People's Party at the end of 2007. He called for an online organization to fight Chinese government online censorship. On May 18, 2008, he was arrested and held for 10 days by the Nanjing police, and after his release, he was fired from his teaching position at Nanjing University, one of the key universities in China.

Sometimes online users are punished merely because they make local government leaders unhappy. In June 2007, for example, an Internet user posted some photos online that showed the luxurious offices of the newly completed city government building in Tengzhou, Shandong province. Municipal officials were worried that the photos might incite criticism of the city government and sent metropolitan police to arrest the Internet user. In November, police in Shanghai raided the home of a blogger and confiscated his computer and equipment after he posted a detailed account of the closure of his magazine earlier that year.

The government's measures, however, are not universally effective. Many Chinese rights activists are now taking their battle for freedom of expression to the Internet. The activists engage in guerrilla-style tactics, posting dissenting opinions and critiques on bulletin boards, chat rooms, and YouTube. They set up quickly moving websites and link them together. These numerous "hacktivists" find ways around the government controls. Because of developments such as this, many observers believe that the battle for the rights of the Chinese people is now online.

Surveillance programs established by the Chinese police are not always capable of completely suppressing online political debate and dissenting opinions. Internet police cannot monitor all online traffic and the numerous Internet cafes. Web activist Wu Wei set up a site in June 2001, but it was quickly shut down. After this incident, Wu and two students started a new website, the Democracy and Freedom

Forum, on free bulletin-board space. So far, the forum has been closed 38 times. During their cat and mouse game, Wu and his colleagues have been harassed by officials. Not all of the "mice" have been so lucky; Liu Di, a student Internet activist known as the "Stainless Steel Mouse," was arrested.

In 2009, China's Internet authorities issued new guidelines for the use of the Web that leaves the level of censorship largely unchanged. Since November 2009, China has closed hundreds of websites and limited its citizens' ability to set up personal websites. In early 2010, the government called for a campaign against pornography, which in fact was targeting "illegal text messages" and "unhealthy content." According to China Mobile, one of the largest cellular providers in the country, text messages would automatically be scanned for keywords provided by the police. The company had to inform the police by forwarding the "illegal and unhealthy" content for police evaluation, and while the evaluation process was ongoing, the cell phone company had to suspend the text-messaging function for those phone numbers.[14]

Many rights groups are demanding better protection of netizens, especially in the areas of freedom of speech and the press. Chinese activists fear that a long, hard road may be ahead before individuals are able to truly express their views and achieve civil liberties online. Many prominent Chinese academics and journalists have spoken out against these restrictive rules. They believe the government should open up more channels in which civic groups and the mass media may engage freely. Officials should fully respect and protect the freedom of the press and the rights of journalists, welcoming rather than fearing the public expression of contentious and diverse views.

Chapter 5

Individual Rights and Collective Interests

This chapter examines the rights of individuals, specifically those concerning privacy, private property, women, and workers, all of which are important civil liberties issues in China today. The right to personal privacy is still new to Chinese society. This is normal for a society based not on Western standards that assert society should serve an individual, but rather on the Eastern notion that citizens are obligated to conform to the culture in which they live. Since China governs a huge population through an intricate hierarchy of communal groups, all citizens are expected to subjugate their individual will to the collective good.

The 1954 Constitution guaranteed the "privacy of correspondence," although government officials continued to open citizens' mail regularly. This sole reference to privacy was struck from the 1975 Constitution and was not reinserted in 1978. This latter document provided that "the citizens' freedom of person and their homes are inviolable." Nevertheless, the Chinese government continues to keep track of what is said in public.

Socioeconomic conditions are an important factor in the status of private or individual rights. The changes in China's social environment and the government's recognition of these factors as having an influence in the development of civil liberties raises a new question: How well does the government protect weaker elements of society, such as rural laborers, women, and children? In recent decades, the country has undergone an unprecedented social transition. Although international views of this transformation vary, there is a general consensus that it can be broken down into three stages. First, it became industrialized, changing from a farming to manufacturing economy. Second, it became urbanized, as more and more people moved into the cities. Third, it has moved away from high birth and death rates. The tremendous social transitions under way in China today have led to the changes in civil liberties and individual rights that are taking place within the constraints of the Chinese government.

PRIVACY, PROPERTY, AND POVERTY

Article 40 of the 1982 Constitution states: "Freedom and privacy of correspondence of citizens of the People's Republic of China are protected by law." However, in practice, the authorities often do not respect the privacy of citizens. After the Xinjiang riots on July 5, 2009, the government blocked telephone and Internet communications between the region and the outside world for five months. Human rights experts have emphasized that China's social changes require the government to protect individual rights and civil liberties further, especially among victims of ongoing industrialization and urbanization. The new land system and privatization of companies have created new economic opportunities, but also widened the gap between the rich and poor.

Industrial and urban areas have changed more rapidly than rural China, which has lost a large population, especially young farmers. The country's farming population has steadily declined since 1978. In the 1960s, farmers composed 84.2 percent of the nation's total workforce. Then, the farming population declined to 67.4 percent in 1978, 55.8 percent in 1988, 44 percent in 1999, and 40.3 percent in 2004. (See Figures 1 and 2a,b) This decrease in the agricultural population resulted from the implementation of the "household production responsibility system" and improvements in farming techniques in the 1980s.

Peasants had long been dissatisfied with the state-owned land system that existed from 1949 to 1978. Productivity was poor, and the country's agricultural industry was at the brink of bankruptcy. In 1978, the government began to redistribute land to households on the condition that a certain amount of output was given to the government through the household production responsibility system. This practice was immediately successful because individual farmsteads regained complete control of their inputs and outputs by simply giving peasants the right to control and manage their productivity. Farmers began to invest in mechanization, irrigation, and other related facilities. These developments freed many peasants from farming, and many either started their own businesses in their hometown or left the countryside to find work in manufacturing in the cities. Some now run chicken farms, cattle ranches, or food-processing factories. Since the 1980s, this activity has resulted in a significant increase in the number of privately owned businesses in both rural and urban areas.

Compared to other areas of Chinese society, notions of private property and privacy, in all regions of the country, have drastically changed in the past 30 years. The Chinese government is now able to recognize the private ownership of property and is willing to protect the right to individual privacy. From 1982 to 1999, the Chinese constitution was revised four times to legalize the status of a progressively larger private sector in China's socialist state economy. In 1982, the constitution recognized "self-employment" merely as a "supplement" to the state economy. In 1988, that was revised to allow the "existence and growth of private economy" and to recognize "private economy" as a "supplement to the socialist state economy." Further revisions in 1993 included allowing the household production responsibility system to replace the people's communes and legalizing the private management of state enterprises. The legal status of the private economy was established and clearly noted in the 1999 amendment 16 to the constitution that stated: "Non-state economy, self-employment, private economy, etc. are an important component in the socialist market economy." For the first time, the socialist state economy was redefined as a socialist *market* economy. As the centralized state economy has declined, the state has lost its central gravity in terms of manpower and resources.

The transition to a market economy has dramatically changed traditional values and attitudes. In 1978, for the first time, the Party Center of the Chinese Communist Party encouraged people to become rich. With the slogan "To Be Rich Is Glorious," the party won the endorsement of the people, particularly the peasants. By substantially retreating from grassroots rural society and loosening control over people's mobility, the government further allowed peasants to take up occupations previously available only to urban residents. Peasants now have two choices: farm to improve their living situation, or leave the village for new opportunities.

The gap between the rich and the poor is widening within Chinese society, especially in rural areas. Social stratification manifests itself as a

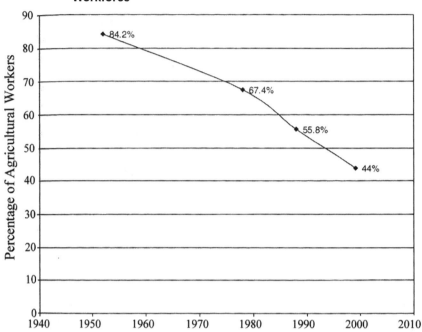

Figure 1. Decreasing Percentage of Agricultural Workers in China's Workforce

new challenge to civil liberties. From 1949 to 1990, Chinese society was fragmented into three major groups: farmers, workers, and cadres. Disparities in political prestige, income, and education were obvious, and the ability of farmers and workers to "narrow the gap" in these areas was severely limited. In the late 1980s, social changes as a result of privatization diminished the boundaries between different social statuses that had previously been clearly and rigidly marked. Since the turn of the century, the rapid change in China's traditional social strata has largely been perceived as beneficial to the healthy growth of its society. It increases opportunities for the general public and helps bring the social mechanisms of choice and reward to the general populace, a norm that did not exist in the past. In the meantime, however, many workers lost their "iron rice bowls," or secured incomes. China's industrialization has been largely based on the low wages paid to workers.

As a result of the economic reforms and the introduction of a market economy, the concepts of commercialism and capitalism are changing the Chinese mind-set. As the population becomes more pragmatic, realistic, and materialistic, many Chinese have come to admire the rich and famous and desire to lead a luxurious lifestyle exclusively concerned with money. They believe that their standard of living and social status depend on the amount of money they have. Another striking feature of China's social hierarchy in the twenty-first century is the rapid polarization of wealth. In 2000, the estimated combined wealth of the top 50 richest entrepreneurs in China was $10 billion. The individual at number 50 was worth $42 million. Based on per capita income differentials, that amount is roughly equivalent to $500 million in the United States. The person at number one, in comparison, had an estimated net worth of $2 billion. The gap between the rich and the poor has widened. In 2003, the National Bureau of Statistics issued an official calculation of 0.375 as its Gini coefficient; by 2004, the Gini coefficient had increased to 0.4725.[1] For China's industrial and agricultural workers, who account for two-thirds of the total population, the average annual wage was well below $500 for 2004.

Rural areas are typically less well off than urban areas. The per capita annual net income of rural households was less than $300 in 2001, compared to a per capita annual disposable income of $812 for those in urban areas. The distribution of wealth is even more uneven for ethnic minorities. The five autonomous regions, where most minority ethnic groups live, accommodate a large proportion of agricultural workers and other lower-income social groups. Within each autonomous region, counties with concentrations of ethnic minorities are at a greater disadvantage. For instance, out of 104 poverty-stricken villages in the Yili prefecture in the Xinjiang Uyghur Autonomous Region, 102 are national minority villages.[2] In Guizhou, another relatively low-income province, 21 of 31 poverty-stricken counties are in minority regions, accounting for half of the total minority population in the province. The poverty line in China is set at 2 yuan RMB ($0.28) a day, or 683 yuan RMB ($97) a year, and that a person does not have enough food and clothing to meet his or her basic needs. It is well below the international standard of poverty of one dollar (7 yuan RMB) a day or $365 (2,555 yuan RMB) a year.

According to official statistics, more than 250 million Chinese people were below the poverty line in 1978. This number was reduced to

42 million by 1998, and to 30.7 million by 2006. An estimated total of 20–28 million people still do not have enough food and clothes. In the rural areas, many peasants do not have a farming job and must leave their hometown to look for other opportunities. In urban areas, more than 20 million residents depend on government and social welfare because they are not able to find a full-time job to support their families. This is partly because agricultural laborers are the most

Figure 2a. Composition of China's Workforce in 1978

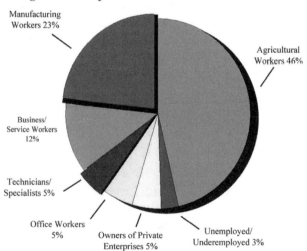

Figure 2b. Composition of China's Workforce in 1999

mobile segment of the population and make constant efforts to squeeze into other social strata within the cities.

MIGRANT LABORERS AND WORKERS' RIGHTS

The problems of China's migrant labors have become serious in terms of their lives and rights. Labor migration from rural to urban areas emerged as a nationwide phenomenon in the late 1980s. By the early 1990s, the number of individuals who had made this move was estimated at approximately 30 million. In the early 2000s, as many as 100 million rural laborers were estimated to be on the move and seeking work in cities and coastal areas, resulting in problems related to employment, housing, public education, health care, transportation, and law enforcement. In the big cities, such as Beijing, Shanghai, Guangzhou, and Tianjin, between two million and four million transients are camped in railway stations and other public places. Neither the city nor the rural governments have any control over them since the central government does not have viable regulations relating to labor issues. The city governments continue to deny permanent residency to these formerly rural residents. This urban/rural segregation has created serious concerns and generated hostility between the government and migrants.

As previously stated, China's industrialization is partly based on the low wages paid to workers, especially migrant workers. Some of these latter workers are treated unfairly, and many are underpaid. Approximately 74 percent of the migrant laborers in 2005 made 580–1,400 yuan RMB (between $80 and $200) a month. Some official estimates suggest that more than 120 million peasants may have left the countryside for the cities as of 2006, leaving behind at least an equal number of peasants who are underemployed in their home rural communities. Since many of the peasants who moved into urban areas cannot find jobs, they have become part of the mobile or "floating" population, a group estimated in the late 1990s to be around 36 million across the country.[3] Aside from these issues, Chinese laborers do not have a unified voice for their own rights and interests. Ethnic, social, gender, and religious diversity have divided Chinese workers in troubling ways.

Females comprise more than 30 percent of all migrant workers in the country. They face numerous challenges in the workplace, including longer working hours, lower wages, and poorer access to safe and sanitary work environments. The children of the migrant workers lack parenting and face serious family problems. There were more than 150,000 urban "street children" in China in 2005, according to state-run media.[4] Many of them were the children of the migrant workers who spend the day on the street. In August 2008, state media reported that the number of children in rural areas left behind by their migrant worker parents totaled 5.8 million.

Both Chinese migrant laborers and full-time workers continue to confront many problems. According to research on the migrant laborers in the city of Wuhan, in central Hubei province, in 2005–2006 approximately 70 percent of these individuals had to work an average of 10.2 hours a day. More than 20 percent worked 13 hours every day. None had health or work-related injury insurance. According to another report published on June 10, 2006, by the World Federation of Trade Unions, the rights of some Chinese manufacturing workers were violated by their employers. These workers were paid below the minimum wage and had to work seven days a week, often 12 to 13 hours a day. Some of these workers did not have one day off during an entire month.[5]

Many workers labor under extremely dangerous conditions. In April 2007, at a steel plant in Liaoning province, 32 workers were killed when nearly 30 tons of molten steel poured onto the shop floor. In August of the same year, 14 migrant workers died and 59 were injured following an aluminum spill at a factory in eastern Shandong province. Coal mining is still the most dangerous profession in China, and throughout the rest of the world. Official statistics show that the number of accidents and fatalities increased from 3,082 in 2000 to 3,790 in 2002 and 4,143 in 2003; in 2004 and 2005, the fatalities reached the horrendous high of approximately 6,000 miners each year. Again according to official statistics, the first quarter of 2007 saw 1,066 coal-mining accidents and 1,792 fatalities. In August 2007, 181 miners died after two coal mines in Xintai, in eastern Shandong province, flooded following torrential rains. The majority of workers who take these types of high-risk jobs are migrant laborers. They make up 90 percent of the miners, 80 percent of construction workers, and almost 100 percent of fireworks manufacturers.

Chinese workers are still forbidden to form independent trade unions. The law does not protect workers' right to strike. The party-controlled All-China Federation of Trade Unions (ACFTU) facilitates government

Rescuers prepare to go into a coal mine to search for stranded miners in Hebi City in central China's Henan province, 2005, after a gas explosion occurred earlier in the day. Thirty four miners were killed by an earlier blast. China's coal mines are the world's deadliest, accounting for about 80 percent of mine fatalities anywhere. There were 5,986 miners killed in 3,341 explosions, fires, and floods in 2005—about the same as in 2004. Most perished at small, often illegal mines that are sometimes little more than holes in the ground. (AP Photo/Xinhua, Yue Yuewei, File.)

policy, but not necessarily the protection of workers' rights. The ACFTU claims to have 209 million members in 1.7 million constituent unions, in 3.6 million enterprises. Human Rights Watch has reported that

> this restriction on legally-sanctioned labor activism, coupled with increasingly intense labor disputes, in which protesting workers have few realistic routes for redress, has contributed to an increasing number of workers taking to the streets and the courts to press claims related to unpaid pensions and wages, child labor, and dangerous working conditions.[6]

According to some social surveys, the current concerns of Chinese workers are health care, government corruption, and housing.[7] Workers who seek the rectification of their situation have organized rallies, strikes, and demonstrations. In 2006, an estimated 80,000 incidents of social unrest and protest took place across the country.

The government has begun to realize the problems plaguing the workplace, including labor relations, the abuse of migrant laborers, discrimination against women, and unsafe working conditions. In May 2007, the Executive Office of the National People's Congress drafted the Act for Employment Promotion of the PRC and sent it out for review and discussion. On June 29, 2007, the NPC passed the Law of Laborer Contracts in order to protect the rights and interests of workers. This new law, which went into effect January 1, 2008, has had a positive impact on labor relations by establishing requirements for employers in areas such as equal work and pay, ending gender and age discrimination, creating healthy working conditions, and providing fair treatment of migrant laborers. The law, however, is too late for those already injured by previous practices.

THE RIGHTS OF WOMEN AND CHILDREN

After the founding of the PRC, the liberation of Chinese women and the abolition of arranged marriages became a top priority for the government. Article 48 of the 1982 Constitution grants women "equal rights with men in all spheres of life" and says they are supposed to receive "equal pay for equal work." During the legal reform of the 1990s, the government updated some of the laws regarding social and economic equality for women. In the following decade, the government further revised the Marriage Law, Law on Population and Family Planning, Regulations for the Administration of Family Planning Technology and Service, Implementation Procedures for the Law on Healthcare for Mothers and Infants, and Regulations for Premarital Healthcare Work. In 2001, the Chinese government promulgated and put into effect the "Outline for the Development of Chinese Women, 2001–2010" and the "Outline for the Development of Chinese Children, 2001–2010." The next year, the State Council revised and implemented the Regulations on Prohibiting the Use of Child Labor, and the Law on the Protection of Women's Rights and Interests was revised in 2004. These efforts show that the Chinese government has begun to pay attention to women's health care, education, employment, marriage, and family issues.

One explanation for these renewed government efforts is the increased involvement by women in politics, especially in all levels of the people's congresses. At the national level, women comprised 20.2 percent of the Tenth NPC, 13.2 percent of its Standing Committee, and 18.8 percent of the vice chairs. According to official reports, at the local level, more than 5,000 women play a leadership role in both party and government offices in provinces, counties, and municipalities in the 2010s.[8]

The government claims that the gender relations and economic equality at workplaces have been improved in recent years. Women make up 38 percent of all those employed in urban areas. The official human rights report indicated that "the proportion of women in primary and secondary industries has been on the decline, while in new industries and technology-intensive fields, the proportion of women has increased."[9] This shift in employment statistics may be the result of more women taking part in educational opportunities. The ratio of women in school at all levels has risen. In 2002, 98.6 percent of all school-age children were enrolled in primary schools, including 98.5 percent of all girls. Females made up 46.7 percent of the high school population and 46.7 percent of four-year colleges.

In 2005, the government amended the Law on the Protection of Women's Rights by including a ban on sexual harassment. In June 2008, a court in Chengdu, in southwestern Sichuan province, sentenced a manager from a high-tech firm to five months in prison for molesting a female employee, marking the first sexual harassment conviction in the country.

Even though there are laws designed to protect women and children, significant problems remain from gender discrimination, violence, human trafficking, and the sex trade. Critics point out that the NPC failed to clearly define domestic violence in its 2005 legislation on the protection of women's rights. The Chinese media have reported an increase of domestic violence, which affects about 30 percent of Chinese families. In its official annual report, the All-China Women's Federation (ACWF) confirmed the increase of the complaints about family problems, many of which were considered domestic violence. The ACWF national headquarters said it received 300,000 complaints in

2007 reporting domestic violence. Its report also stated that a quarter of the 400,000 divorce cases that year were due to family violence.[10]

Even though there have been some efforts made by the government to stop the sex trade, several million women are involved in prostitution in the country. According to official statistics, 94,687 cases involving prostitution were investigated by police in 2007. The government provided medical treatment and conducted a general survey of gynecological diseases.

By the end of 2002, 68 percent of unmarried pregnant women and 90.1 percent of married ones had undergone prenatal examinations. As of 2002, the country had 3,067 maternity and childcare facilities, and 97.2 percent of rural areas had adopted modern midwifery techniques.

The government has also recognized the problem of human trafficking that is taking place in China. The state has begun to crack down on the abduction and selling of women and children, as well as other criminal offenses perpetrated against these members of society. According to official reports, local police rescued more than 2,000 abducted women and children in 2003. In 2006, the high court in southern Fujian province reportedly upheld criminal sentences for a group of men convicted of trafficking more than 130 individuals to various countries from 2004 to 2006; the three ringleaders of the group were sentenced to jail terms of 13, 8, and 5 years. On May 9, 2007, six parents who lost their children went to the provincial television station in Henan for help. They believed that their boys, between the ages of 8 and 13, had been kidnapped to sell to the illegal coal mines in Shanxi, a neighboring province. After the reporters' investigation, the station broadcasted a program entitled "Tragedy of the Child Laborers" on June 5. Following this, the station received letters from 400 more parents who had lost their children. On June 25, the state police from Henan and Shanxi provinces raided the illegal mines and rescued 532 slave laborers, including 109 children. Most of the children had been abducted at bus stops or train stations and then sold for 500 yuan RMB ($70) per child.

Although Chinese law prohibits the employment of children under the age of 16, a U.S. State Department report points out that the Chinese government has not adopted a "comprehensive policy to combat child labor" and concludes that child labor remains a "persistent problem."[11] According to a report by the World Federation of Trade

A girl works at a brick kiln at Liuwu Village in Yuncheng in China's Shanxi province, 2007. China arrested two labor bureau officials for their alleged links to slave labor in brick kilns, amid reports that kiln bosses were hiding child laborers and charging ransoms for their release. (AP Photo/Color China Photo, File.)

Unions in June 2006,[12] some manufacturing companies hire child laborers during the summer and winter breaks. One such company employed more than 20 children between the ages of 12 and 15 for full-time jobs. These employees were paid much lower than the minimum wage and had to work as many hours a day as adult workers. Child labor was reportedly uncovered in low-skill manufacturing sectors such as toys, textiles, and shoes. In October 2008, in central Hubei province, the municipal government of the capital city of Wuhan launched a campaign to crack down on child labor in sweatshops in the local garment, silk screening, zipper, and mop factories.

As in most societies, child labor, human trafficking, prostitution, drug addiction, and domestic violence and abuse are entrenched and very resistant to change. The Ministry of Public Security has estimated that 10,000 women and children are abducted and sold each year, and some nongovernmental organizations estimate that between 20,000 and 30,000 were trafficked annually. The ministry reported about 2,500 trafficking cases during 2008, although experts claimed the number was much higher. Between February and July 2008, police in Guangdong province reportedly handled 33 trafficking cases and arrested 57 suspects involved in the trafficking in persons, 15 of whom were foreign nationals.

After China globalized its economy and improved its trade with bordering countries, the human trafficking became internationalized. In November 2008, police in southeastern Fujian province investigated a cross-border trafficking case in which 18 Vietnamese women were brought from Vietnam and sent to China's border provinces, including Yunnan and Guangxi, and were reportedly sold into marriages in rural communities for 20,000 to 30,000 yuan RMB (approximately $3,000–4,400) each. In southwestern Guizhou province, state media reported that courts heard a case involving 30 suspects accused of trafficking more than 80 women over a four-year period from Guizhou to Shanxi, Fujian, Zhejiang, and other eastern provinces. The women were led to believe they were being provided employment, but instead were unwillingly moved to rural areas for forced marriages. Some international rights groups have concluded that China's trafficking problems partially result from the country's social stratification and family planning policy—the "one-child policy"—to which we turn now.

THE ONE-CHILD POLICY

China's family planning and birth control policy, known as the "one-child policy," began in 1979 in an attempt by the government to solve the overpopulation problem. This policy has become one of the most prominent ways in which the state intrudes in family life. In 2000, the CCP's Central Committee and the State Council issued a joint statement entitled "Decision on Strengthening Population and Family Planning Work." In 2001, the NPC passed the Legislation on Population and Birth Planning, which legalized the population policy of controlling population growth and implemented the basic state policy of family planning in an all-around way.

The legislation suggested late marriage and late childbearing and advocated the continuing practice of one child per couple. The law set the marriage age for women at 20 and for men at 22.

A man walks past a roadside sculpture which promotes China's one-child policy, in Beijing. Enforcement of the one-child policy, introduced in the 1970s to control China's population growth, has been relaxed in recent years. New regulations have been introduced allowing many rural couples, and some urban couples to have larger families. (AP Photo/Greg Baker.)

It continues to be illegal for a couple to have a second child in most urban areas, and in some of the ethnic minority areas where the parents may have a second child, the government restricts the rights of these parents to decide *when* they can have the second child. It is illegal in almost all provinces for a single woman to have a baby.

Since the implementation of the one-child family planning policy, the average fertility rate has dropped from six children per family in the 1970s, to two per family in 2000, and to just 1.44 per family in 2002. The government views this as a success and claims that 250 million births have been avoided. It also asserts that the decline in the growth rate has improved health care among women and children. The reduction in the number of births is largely attributable to the prevalence of contraceptive use and the large number of induced abortions that have occurred as long-term birth control has been made both more widely available and compulsory.

The government changed the one-child policy in September 2002 to permit ethnic minorities and Chinese who live in remote and less populated rural areas to have a second child. The new Family Planning Law allows provinces and municipalities to establish local regulations regarding having a second child. Some local governments already had laws to that effect. For example, the Anhui provincial government recently passed regulations that permit 13 categories of couples to apply to have a second child, while some can have a third or more. In other provinces, some villages have abolished birth permits (a quota system) and let couples decide on their own when to have a baby. Even some cities now grant single-children parents the right to have a second child, but may require that the births are at least five years apart.

One explanation for the stabilization of the population is the improvement of public education. Education has a direct effect on the desired family size of Chinese women. Illiterate women desire 3.1 children on average, those literate with below a middle school education hope for 2.6, middle-school-educated women want 2.4, and those with a high school education or above desire only two children. Approximately 58 percent of illiterate women have not discussed family planning with their husbands, while the equivalent percentages for those with less than a middle school education, a middle school education, and high school or above are 42, 35, and 29, respectively. In addition, for these same four categories of women, the proportions who were unaware of modern contraception were 15.9, 4.8, 3.0, and 1.1 percent, respectively.

In 1949, 90 percent of Chinese women were illiterate. In 1978, the female illiteracy rate had dropped to 31 percent, and by 1997 it had reached 23.2 percent. According to official statistics, Chinese women had an average of elementary education through public schools by 1998. Female students increased from 26.5 percent of the middle school population in 1950 to 46.5 percent in 1998. The proportion of female college students in regular institutions of higher education rose from 19 percent in 1949 to 38.3 percent in 1998.[13]

Chinese women have begun to reshape their perceived self-interest. During the 1950s through the 1970s, children left school early to work for their families. During the 1990s and later, however, China reached the stage of development where children became increasingly expensive and contributed little in economic terms. They go to school for many years, then to work and marriage when they establish separate households.

Another explanation for the success of China's one-child policy has been strict government enforcement. After 1979, having more than one child was punishable by fines and jail time. Chapter 5 of the 2001 legislation lists all the punishments for those who do not follow the laws of family planning. The first punishment is to pay a heavy fine of about 3,000 yuan RMB ($500), which is equivalent to an average one-year income in rural areas, plus the loss of all benefits. Another consequence for a couple bearing a child outside the plan could be the immediate end of their career or professional development. Connecting the young people's careers to their family planning provides a powerful incentive, since most young couples do not want to risk their future livelihood. The third potential punishment for those who fail to follow the plan is administrative discipline, including demotion, relocation, or even termination of employment. Since employers and officials at all levels are subject to rewards or penalties based on their efforts in reaching the population control goals, their own promotion and pay raises depend on meeting population targets set up by their superiors. In some cases, the employers have fired pregnant female employees before they deliver their babies to avoid having a bad record of family planning for their company or school.

The population control program continues to negatively affect Chinese women. Violent actions, such as forced abortions and sterilization, have been taken against many women who did not follow the government's one-child policy. Some activists who asked for more protection of women's rights have been attacked by government officials and the police.

In September 2005, Chen Guangcheng, a blind activist in the city of Linyi, Shandong province, was grabbed and forced into the back of an undercover police vehicle, dragged and beaten, and threatened with charges of spying because he had revealed the abuse of rural women in the name of family planning policies. Chen was told by one of the officials that he may have violated the law by passing news information to the foreign media, which was equated with providing intelligence to foreign countries, for which the maximum penalty is life in prison. "The main purpose was to threaten me," Chen told reporters after his release. During his kidnapping, officials called in his family to persuade him to give up his activism. Later, the deputy mayor of Linyi stated the reason for the abduction was to protect him from "being used by the foreign media." Chen's wife, Yuan Weijing, had helped her husband during his activities. The authorities took away her passport so she could not leave the country to accept a human rights prize on behalf of her husband. Then she was arrested by police and given a three-year sentence for reporting family planning abuses.[14]

The single-child policy results in selective abortions and even female infanticide. In a traditional society like China, preference for sons has deep cultural roots. Actually, preferential treatment toward males is part of the Confucian value system. Girls are not welcome in families; Chinese mothers are usually under a great pressure to have a boy. After the one-child policy was implemented, some women have tried to terminate their pregnancy if they knew they were having a female baby. The Law on the Protection of Juveniles forbids infanticide, but evidence has shown that it still occurs, including selective abortion of female fetuses and the termination of female babies' lives whenever a doctor may be cooperative; one group of doctors was charged with infanticide. This is a significant contribution to the gender imbalance in mainland China, where there was, in 2005, a 118:100 ratio of male to female babies.[15] According to a government estimate released on February 28, 2008,[16] the male-to-female sex ratio at birth was 120:100, and many cities have more than 125 boys for every 100 girls.

Some international rights groups have suggested that, as Freedom House puts it, "the Chinese government should increase planning and resources that are devoted to enforcing constitutional provisions and existing laws that protect the rights of workers, women, and children."[17] Officials must guarantee civil liberties and punish those who violate them. The state can fund the comprehensive social security system for employees, including medical insurance, childbirth leave, labor protection, unemployment benefits, and retirement pensions. China must narrow the gap between the rich and poor while improving the standard of living for all people throughout the country. In order to accomplish this, however, it must first solve the problem of poverty.

Chapter 6

Rights of the Accused

The Chinese government realizes the importance of a civil society and a country governed by the rule of law, under which individuals and organizations are treated and held equally responsible. From 2006 to 2009, the Party Center sped up legal reform to achieve its goal of making the rule of law "the principal tool to govern the country."[1] New laws were adopted on a wide range of issues: property rights, the administration of lawyers, and labor relations in 2007; the administration of lawyers and the handling of emergencies in 2008; and access to public records and incidental responsibilities in 2009. These reforms have had a strong impact on the criminal justice system, and tremendous changes have taken place in courtrooms, law firms, and prisons. Because of a societal environment that is increasingly supportive of legal reform, more and more people have become conscious of their rights as citizens. The concept of using legal means to protect these rights has made significant progress.

This development has had a very important impact on China's legal system and the state as a whole. Two interesting, if somewhat contradictory, trends can be observed: first, the separation of the law from the state; and second, bringing the state back in to reinforce the new rule of law. The former restrains the state's power, while the latter presses the government to use its power to pursue justice. Both trends, however, appear to serve the purpose of promoting constitutional rights over the state itself. Growing numbers of people now turn to legal sources for assistance in solving problems with their employer or the authorities. By 2000, the Chinese courts were handling more cases than ever before, with those studying the subject noting that the country was facing a "litigation explosion."

In the meantime, though, little structural change has been made within the constitution. As a result, the constitution has some intrinsic deficiencies. For example, the enforcement of court decisions is limited, and few legal sanctions exist for violators. One of the international human rights organizations has pointed out, "The Party's continued dominance over, and interference with, judicial institutions, as well as the weak and inconsistent enforcement of judicial decisions means that, overall, the legal system remains vulnerable to arbitrary interference and remains a tool of the CCP."[2]

Moreover, it is difficult to implement the rule of law because party leaders and government officials are supposedly morally superior and above the law. China's legal tradition has always emphasized that rights are not derived from the "inherent dignity" of being human, or "natural rights," but are rather granted from the political authority as "legal rights" or "discretionary entitlement." Logically, because rights and civil liberties are granted by the authorities, they can also be withdrawn by them. Currently, the dominant group uses the laws as a flexible means to maintain its position and secure its interests. The country is still ruled by the law of the Chinese Communist Party and its government.

This chapter focuses on the rights of the criminally accused by examining the criminal justice system, including legal processes, court procedures, the use of force, and prosecution and referral to procurators. It will also focus on the rights of citizens as stated in the law, such as freedom from unreasonable government searches, freedom of the accused from unfair interrogation and from being forced to testify against themselves, the right of the accused to have a lawyer in criminal proceedings, the right to a fair trial and appellate review, and freedom from cruel and unusual punishment. This chapter also identifies major problems facing court and procuratorial reforms and the opposition from law enforcement to these ongoing judicial changes. It provides a balanced perspective on court reform efforts and the challenges of the Chinese judicial system.

NEW LAW AND ORDER

China's judicial branch includes state and public security, prosecutors, courts, judicial organizations, and the prison system. Public security is composed of armed police as well as those responsible for the investigation of criminal activities and the prison administration. The prosecution is conducted by the procurators who exercise their authority through the courts. Judicial organizations include those of lawyers, public notaries, and arbitrators. The highest judicial organ is the Supreme People's Court (or the Supreme Court) and the Supreme People's Procuratorates (or the Supreme Procuratorates).

The most important aim of China's judicial system is to control society and regulate social behavior, not to define and protect individual rights. This idea is best illustrated in the country's administrative laws. During the reforms that began in 1978, the administrative sources of the central government's power have been greatly reduced, thus making total control over society unsustainable. As the state retreats from its domination, a more pluralistic society is able to develop. This happened first in nonpolitical areas, such as popular culture and social life, and has since spread to other areas. One evident consequence is an increase in the people's economic, social, and cultural freedoms. In this process, a large part of the central government's administrative powers has either been transferred to local governments or replaced by other forms of control mechanisms, such as administrative laws.

Administrative Laws

In the last 20 years, according to Article 89 of the 1982 Constitution, the State Council as the central administrative body has been granted the legislative competence and jurisdiction to enact administrative laws. In 2001, China was accepted by the World Trade Organization and joined the international market of trade, finance, insurance, transportation, telecommunication, and other sectors. The globalization of the Chinese economy required the country to align its trade regulations and business codes with international standards. To promote China's economy and win world trade, the Chinese government has made many revisions of its laws to meet international rules. By 2004, administrative laws and regulations accounted for more than 60 percent of all laws in China. The State Council alone has issued more than 800 of these. Among the 5,000 local laws and regulations, administrative laws account for more than half. The whole administrative system has been rebuilt according to these new rules, regulations, and laws, thereby making it more regulative, transparent, and accountable.

The Tiananmen National Flag Escort of the People's Armed Police. (Macmaniac/ Dreamstime.com.)

Among the most important laws, the Administrative Litigation Law, the Administrative Punishment Law, and the State Compensation Law have begun to provide citizens with judicial resources when their rights are violated by the government's actions.

These new laws have given rise to a significant judicial practice: people can sue the government for its wrongdoing. Although these rights might still be rather symbolic, they establish the notion of judicial review of administrative acts and create a starting point for the further use of laws to check government power. For example, the Administrative Permission Law sets legal restrictions and establishes a judicial review mechanism over the government's administrative power of granting licenses and permissions. All of these are a departure from China's long tradition of centralized and unaccountable power. According to official statistics, 101,510 administrative lawsuits were filed against the government in 2007, slightly more than in the previous year. In the first five months of 2008, prosecutors filed and investigated 20,294 cases of embezzlement, bribery, or dereliction of duty.[3] From December 2002 to June 2007, the Party Center reported that 518,484 party members were punished for breaking party discipline. From November 2007 to November 2008, 151,000 party and government officials were disciplined.

The administrative law regime does, however, have some obvious flaws. For example, the priority of this system is to strengthen the government's governing capacity rather than monitor and check its power. Its main goal is to promote compliance through the use of administrative agencies with substantive laws rather than to establish procedural safeguards for individuals. Thus, administrative laws are often made primarily to favor the responsible government agencies, rather than ordinary citizens. From content to procedure, administrative laws have inadequately taken into account public opinion or citizens' rights, and they are mostly concerned with improving management. The committees of the CCP and governments at the provincial, county, and municipal levels have the final say on local court procedures, judges' appointments and promotions, and decisions on whether a trial will be public or closed. Moreover, in administrative lawmaking, the lack of openness and transparency reflects inadequate procedural justice and the restriction of a citizen's right to information. Because of this, many practical rules that could be made to protect civil rights actually enable their restriction. All of these factors have made it difficult to sufficiently protect citizens' legal rights against government misconduct.

Citizens must also go through immense obstacles to access legal services and justice at the local level, particularly since most cases are against local authorities and corrupt officials in their hometowns. These suits are often brought forward because of bribery, kickbacks, abuse of power, and mismanagement. The Party Center encourages the people to go through the legal system to address their grievances, in order to avoid public demonstrations and even riots. In recent years, waves of lawsuits have been submitted to courts across the country.

Lawlessness and Endless Lawsuits

The courts are not ready to shift from the rule of the party to that of the law for three reasons. The first is that the lack of professionals in both judicial and legal services has enabled an inadequate system to develop. From the beginning of the economic reform in 1978 through the 1980s, the legal system was still in the middle of its recovery. In 1979, for example, the Ministry of Justice reopened after having been closed for 20 years. The country had only four law schools in 1987 and only 25 law departments in universities across the nation. Because of this, the country had only 26,000 lawyers, at a time when at least 200 death sentences were being carried out every month. By 1994, the number of attorneys had increased to 70,000, but the country had 3.85 million legal cases a year. As a result, many defendants did not have legal aid or a chance for appeal. This lack of judicial assistance was particularly egregious in cases that could result in capital punishment, and the accused were often denied a meaningful appeal and not uncommonly executed the day of their conviction. In 1995, only 6 percent of Chinese judges had four-year college degrees, as a law degree was not necessary. By 2000, this number increased, but was still only 20 percent.

The second reason for the slow development of the rule of law is internal problems in judicial organs, such as the corruption that has plagued the legal system. Police, prosecutors, and even judges have taken bribes or given personal favors to let criminals go free or reduce their sentences.

The third reason for the incompetence of the judicial system is the lack of professionalism, including local protectionism, personal connections, and the lack of legal aid and due process. Abuses continued through the 1980s, including police brutality, torture of prisoners, forced confessions, arbitrary arrest and detention, and extrajudicial killings.

Although the judicial system was not ready, more and more lawsuits have been submitted to the courts. The courts reported hearing 5.85 million cases in 2000, almost 2 million more than the number heard in 1994.[4] In 2003, the courts concluded the investigation of 634,953 criminal first-instance cases, 57,505 cases involving national security, 184,018 cases of personal rights violations, and 278,969 cases involving property infringement. The same year, the courts investigated 88,050 administrative lawsuits. The courts in 2003 also investigated 3,124 state compensation cases, ultimately awarding 89.7 million yuan RMB ($12.6 million). All this, coupled with the strict enforcement of the law by public security bodies, has served to help the victims of illegal activities.

Between 2004 and 2006, commercial arbitration cases increased annually by more than 20 percent. In 2000, these totaled 5.38 million cases, including 560,111 criminal cases, 4.37 million civil cases, and 86,614 administrative cases. Labor arbitration more than quintupled between 1996 and 2004, and in 2000 reached a total of 469,545; of these, 86,619 were criminal, 363,522 civil, and 19,404 administrative. During the first decade of the 2000s, there was a modest fluctuation in the number of cases heard in the courts. For example, 5.58 million were brought forward in 2002, including 5.1 million commercial and 474,910 labor cases. In 2004, this number dropped to 5.54 million, but it rose again in 2006 to 5.7 million.[5]

Court Reforms

The court system in China has four levels, with the Supreme Court in Beijing at the top. The courts at higher levels oversee the administration of those at lower levels, including the higher people's courts, intermediate people's courts, and basic people's courts. The first of these three is at the provincial level. The intermediate courts are at the county and municipal levels, governed by the higher courts. The basic courts are in counties, towns, and municipal districts. Each court level has a president and several vice presidents, while each individual court has judges, assistant judges, and members of judicial committees.

In late 2005, the Supreme Court created a five-year plan designed to strengthen the courts. The plan laid out 50 goals, including the improvement of court finances, the appointment of judges, and the reform of procedures for the prosecution of capital cases. Furthermore, the plan sought to break the link with local authorities, who usually control court appointments and judges through the annual budget. Some courts have instituted an important innovation and have begun looking to other courts and judges in deciding difficult cases rather than to party superiors in their local governments.

Judges are more qualified than they were in the past. By mid-2005, for the first time, more than 50 percent of Chinese judges had college degrees.[6] This was a substantial increase from the 6 percent in 1995 and 20 percent in 2000. These changes were a result of a new requirement in 2002 that stated all new judges must have a bachelor's degree. That same year, the Supreme Court also instructed all sitting judges below the age of 40 that they must get a college degree within five years or risk losing their jobs; judges at the age of 50 or older may stay at the court without a college education, but they must complete a legal training course. As a result, most judges today, particularly at higher levels in major cities, now possess bachelor's or postgraduate degrees. Nevertheless, they are not all from four-year universities. Many judges completed work through evening classes, junior colleges, distance learning programs, or correspondence courses—and not necessarily in law.

New Chinese judges are also now required to pass a national bar exam that, when given in 2005, was successfully completed by just 14 percent of the examinees. Those who entered the profession before 2002, however, do not need to pass the test. Neither do court presidents, who tend to be the most powerful figures in the court. Despite not having to be judges,[7] court presidents always take part in the decisions of major or sensitive cases. As growing numbers of court clerks obtain an education, they are developing professional identities, thus giving a new role and popular attention to the judicial system.

The courts have also increased their transparency to improve judicial fairness. Except for those prescribed by the law as unsuitable for public hearing, first-instance cases—those being heard for the first time—may face a public trial. For appeals, the rate of open court sessions has also increased. While in court, both prosecutors and defense lawyers present their evidence, conduct cross-examinations, and engage in debate on the spot. These efforts have avoided closed trials and behind-door deals and increased the rate of judges' decisions announced in court.

While judicial independence is essential for the fair and impartial adjudication of cases, this principle is largely compromised by the structure of the court system. All levels of the judicial system are answerable to the National People's Congress and other party apparatuses, which certainly reduces judicial autonomy. The failure to reform the system of appointing and removing judges and presidents continues to act as a major obstruction to any strengthening of the courts. Similarly, their promotion, rewards, and penalties are also decided by the CCP.

The presidents in most courts, especially at higher levels, are party members. The CCP dominates court adjudication committees, and court presidents, not presiding court judges, often make the final decisions. Because of the party's interference in the judicial process, politically motivated or influenced trials continue to take place. In two of 2004's high-profile "economic crime" cases against Shanghai's Zhou Zhengyi and Guangzhou's *Nanfang Dushibao* (Southern Metropolis Daily), distinctly different verdicts were given. Zhou, who had personal connections to Shanghai's local party officials, received a very light sentence. The editor of the newspaper, which had openly reported on the SARS epidemic and offended local party officials in Guangzhou, received an unreasonably severe punishment.

Besides the courts, political institutions such as the Chinese Communist Youth League, All-China Federation of Trade Unions, and ACWF also engage in dispute resolution and mediation. The People's Mediation Committee is a part of the judicial system and is used to settle litigation outside of the courts. The number of cases seen by this organization has decreased in recent years, from its peak at 5.03 million in 2000 to 4.64 million in 2002 and 4.22 million in 2004. Letters and visits to the courts, however, have fluctuated up and down in recent years. More than 9 million grievances were raised in this manner in 2000. This number dropped to 3.66 million in 2002, but then increased to 4.22 million in 2004.

POLICE, PROSECUTION, AND PUNISHMENT

In China, criminal laws came late and always enjoyed a preeminent status. From 1949 to 1979, the purpose of criminal law was primarily to maintain social and political order through punishment, even though it had a positive impact on the protection of people's rights when a lot of crimes were punished. The criminal law also had another function—to educate. Since the reform movement began, however, mechanisms that protect the rights of individuals have been inserted into the judicial process. Through the addition of criminal laws, these mechanisms strengthen and amplify constitutional guarantees by providing more detail to the procedural and institutional framework through which the enforcement or implementation of constitutional rights is accomplished. For example, the Criminal Law of 1979 implemented the protection of personal freedom by making it an offense to unlawfully detain or search a person and prescribing a punishment for the offender. The Law of Criminal Procedure of 1979 and the Arrest and Detention Act were issued by the Ministry of Justice to regulate arrest and detention procedures.

These laws were amended in 1996–1997 and included some new important principles, such as "conviction and penalty according to the law," "equality of everyone before the law," and the idea that "the severity of penalty should be commensurate with the offender's crime and due criminal liabilities."[8] In 2003, the Supreme Court formulated 20 documents that offered a judicial interpretation of criminal, civil, and administrative law enforcement. Among them was "Interpretations of Some Questions Related to the Concrete Application of the Law in Handling Criminal Cases That Impair the Prevention and Control of the Sudden Onset of Infectious Diseases and Other Disasters." Tracts such as this provide important interpretation and more practical details concerning the legitimate rights of citizens.

In 2003, the Chinese police cracked 2.3 million criminal cases. The Chinese government will often launch "strike hard" campaigns against crime. During these times, the police vigorously combat crime, including organized and gang-related offenses, murder, rape, kidnapping, and other serious violent acts. These campaigns result in severe punishments and mass executions. The public generally supports these harsh measures. Law enforcement officials continue to conduct illegal searches and to utilize extended detention, torture, and forced confessions.

Detention and the Reeducation Through Labor System

Some procedural elements of the justice system have been introduced in an obvious attempt to conform to international standards. The Supreme Court urges judges to "pay more attention to evidence and treat confessions with more skepticism."[9] Article 125 of the 1982 Constitution guarantees public trials, although an accompanying provision is a vague exception for cases involving "special circumstances"; many cases fall into this category and are deemed inaccessible even to family members of the accused. Article 12 of the new Criminal Procedure Law recognizes the principle of presumed innocence with distinctive wording: "No one should be convicted as guilty before the people's court passes a ruling according to law." Another publicized move in criminal justice is to replace the highly politicized charge of "counterrevolution" with the less sensational accusation of "jeopardizing state security."

China's judicial process has been moving away from the "inquisitorial" system toward a combined approach called "inquisitorial and adversarial." Criminal justice based on these two principles is still inadequately appreciative of due process and procedural justice and contains very few remedial provisions concerning measurable legal consequences. In this sense, China still focuses more on substantive than procedural justice.

In China, police can arrest and detain suspects with their administrative detention powers and without warrants from a court. Court approval is not needed for a formal arrest as long as police can obtain approval from the procurators after detention. Under the law, police can hold detainees for up to 37 days before formally placing them under arrest or releasing them. The criminal law also allows police and prosecutors to detain persons up to seven months before any conclusion of investigating their cases. In routine criminal cases, police often detain individuals without notification of their family members. After a suspect is arrested, the individual doesn't know how long he or she will be held by police.[10] The Supreme Procuratorate has acknowledged continuing widespread abuse in law enforcement through excessive detention and mistreatment.

In the Tibetan Autonomous Region, for example, authorities continue to abusively suppress religious groups and political dissidents. Lengthy detention, torture, and extrajudicial killings of Tibetan religious leaders are still common occurrences. Several released prisoners complained that they were beaten or electrically shocked by police officers when they were in jail, and many believed that their confinements had been prolonged. Some also reported that their relatives were pressured by authorities to use bribes to secure their release.

After the March 14, 2008, riots in Lhasa, official state media reported that many Tibetans were arrested "arbitrarily" by authorities. The media confirmed the detentions of 4,434 persons in March and April. These protesters were held without notifications for a significantly long period. Their families had no information about their conditions in detention since there was no official notification about their arrests, and no family visits were allowed. Nevertheless, on May 26, 2008, the family of one of the detainees, Paltsal Kyab, received information from the local police station that he had died in custody. Kyab had participated in a March 17 protest and was arrested in April. Police said that he died from kidney and stomach problems, but his family said that he was a healthy young man at the time of his arrest. Although his family never had a chance to see his body, some witnesses who did said that Kyab's body "was covered with bruises and burn blisters."[11]

During detention, especially in the pretrial period, torture remains prevalent, as policemen, detectives, and armed police continue to make use of the practice. In China, 99 percent of defendants admit to the charges brought against them.

Another controversial institution in China is the Reeducation Through Labor (RTL) system. The RTL system is unique to China. The Public Security Bureau in the cities and provinces and local police can arrest someone for a minor offense and, without trial, put that person in a prison labor camp for up to four years. The practice was adopted in 1957 to target counterrevolutionaries and their family members, who worked in law-enforcement-owned factories or farms as manual laborers to rid them of "deviant" thoughts and attitudes. In 1979, the State Council decreed supplementary regulations regarding the system, and in a 1980 document, it combined forced labor education and detention-investigation into a single practice known as RTL. In 2003, the Ministry of Justice, based on the Law on Prisons, formulated and implemented the Regulations on Reform through Reeducation in Prisons.

Thereafter, the government, through various administrative regulations and judicial interpretations, created informal rules that expanded RTL to cover a wide range of offenses, targeting everyone from counterrevolutionaries and "antiparty, antisocialist" elements to "drug dealers, political and religious dissidents, prostitutes, people who sabotage railway transportation, and members of regressive sects." According to official sources, the annual average number of prisoners sent to RTL camps through the 1980s was 870,000. In total, more than 20 laws and regulations have been passed that govern RTL. The practice, in fact, violates the constitution, the Criminal Procedure Law, and the International Covenant on Civil and Political Rights. A report by Freedom House in 2007 indicated that sentences under the RTL were "even stiffer than those given under criminal law" and that detainees in related facilities "face torture and harsh conditions."[12]

Prosecutions and Procurements

Prosecutors in China still lack independence. A prosecutorial hierarchy called the "people's procuratorates" runs parallel to the court system. At the top is the Supreme People's Procuratorate (or Supreme Procuratorate) in Beijing. Lower levels consist of the higher, intermediate, and basic people's procuratorates. The first are in provinces, autonomous regions, and special municipalities. The intermediate level also exercises authority in those areas, but principally works at the prefecture level. Basic procuratorates are in counties, towns, and municipal districts. Aside from these three standard levels, special procuratorates deal with issues that affect the military, railroad transportation, and forestry. Procurators serve as prosecutors and district attorneys. They are limited to two consecutive terms that run concurrently with the National People's Congress or local people's congresses, the bodies that control their appointment, promotion, and removal.

The Supreme Procuratorate also set up 75 centers at large prisons to provide services through representative offices. That year, the same body held an investigation of complaints by prisoners. Procuratorial bodies have strengthened the supervision of law enforcement by examining situations where the law was not properly carried out, enforcement was weak, or justice was avoided. In 2000, procuratorial offices approved the arrest of 635,000 of 720,000 suspects and filed public charges against 610,000 of them.

In recent years, procuratorial bodies have paid special attention to political scandals, corruption, and mismanagement in the government and the party. In 2005–2006, more than 6,000 officials were investigated, detailed, and sentenced by the prosecutors. One of the major cases was the arrest and sentencing of CCP Politburo member and Shanghai party committee secretary Chen Liangyu in 2006. Chen was charged with corruption and misuse of the city's pension fund. The Shanghai party committee and city government put pressure on the prosecution of Chen's case, including a threat to remove the chief prosecutor from his office. But the prosecutor won the case, and Chen was dismissed from all of his positions in the party and city government in 2007. Then the court agreed with the prosecutor to relocate the case from Shanghai to the northern city of Tianjin, where in November 2008, Chen was convicted and sentenced to 18 years in prison by the Tianjin court.

Chen Liangyu, Shanghai's Communist Party secretary, attends the Chief Justices of the Supreme Court meeting of the Shanghai Cooperation Organization (SCO) in 2006, in Shanghai, China. Chen was dismissed for alleged corruption, the highest level official to be axed in more than a decade as President Hu Jintao moves to consolidate his power. Chinese characters on top read "Shanghai." (AP Photo/Eugene Hoshiko.)

Torture and Conviction

Torture, abuse, and insulting of prisoners are frequently reported in China, even though the law theoretically bans physical abuse of detainees, police brutality, and mistreatment of prisoners. In 1988, China ratified the United Nations Convention against Torture, and in 1998, it signed the International Covenant on Civil and Political Rights. In 2002, the Chinese government promulgated "Provisions on Procedures of Handling Administrative Cases by Public Security

Organs" in an effort to tighten law enforcement procedures, strengthen internal supervision of security agencies, deal with human rights violations involving the obtaining of confessions through the use of torture, diminish the abusive use of guns, and limit other coercive measures. In 2003, the Supreme Court, Supreme Procuratorate, and Ministry of Public Security jointly issued "Notice on the Strict Enforcement of the Criminal Procedure Law, and on the Conscientious Prevention and Correction of Extended Detention." In order to facilitate this, the Supreme Procuratorate established special phone numbers and e-mail addresses to receive complaints and reports of extended detention. According to its phone and case records, by the end of 2003, the government had corrected 25,736 cases, including 259 cases of illegal detention, 29 of illegal searches, 52 of extorting confessions by torture, 32 concerning the abuse of prisoners and detainees, and many cases of illegal extended detentions.[13]

According to the statistics of some international human rights organizations, at least 930 cases of police torture took place in 2006. In Tunchang County, Hainan province, Li Jiyi was arrested for stealing a police motorcycle. Four policemen took turns beating Li, and the next morning the 28-year-old died of torture while still in custody. In Guangzhou, the local police arrested Li Tianrong, a manager of a trading company in Lanzhou, in northwestern Gansu province. The police suspected he was involved in business fraud and tortured him for a confession. Li refused, and he was illegally detained for 757 days and continually tortured. Without any evidence, the police finally arrested him two years later. On December 16, 2006, Chen Mingshen, a 73-year-old retired policewoman, was arrested because she was suspected of being a member of Falun Gong. For seven months, she was tortured and not allowed any family visits before finally dying in the local police station.

The UN Commission on Human Rights special rapporteur found many cases of torture and other cruel, inhuman, or degrading treatments during a 2005 visit to China. From time to time, the media and Internet users exposed misconduct and excessive use of force against detainees or prisoners. In 2003, the media reported the death of Sun Zhigang in a police detention center. As a newly graduated college student majoring in graphic design, Sun was beaten by security guards in the city of Guangzhou simply because he did not carry his temporary residential card and quarreled with the police. Because of situations such as this, the public does not perceive agents of law enforcement as being respectful of human rights.

The Death Penalty

Provisions that provide for the most serious legal punishment, the death sentence, have increased in number. In 1979, the Criminal Code included 26 crimes punishable by death. A 1995 amendment raised this number to 60. The 1997 Criminal Law then increased the number of "absolute" cases of the death penalty to 68, including homicide, rape, robbery, bombings, and economic crimes. Capital punishment for some crimes, including tax fraud, passing fake negotiable notes, and the illegal "pooling" of funds, is unique to the Chinese judicial system. The government, however, claims that this level of punishment is necessary to combat increasing corruption. The 1997 legislation also further decentralized the appeals process, giving final authority to the provincial supreme courts rather than to the national Supreme Court. Both of these measures have increased the number of executions in recent years. Often, executions are carried out on the same day as the sentencing.[14]

The authorities' attempts to expand the scale of capital punishment reflect the government's concerns over increasing crime. This effort is inconsistent with the global trend of seeking to reduce or eliminate the death sentence altogether, despite China having signed two key international human rights treaties in the 2000s that included articles against the sentence. The country leads the world in executions, accounting for over 70 percent of criminals executed in the world every year, and in 2005 had 1,770 put to death.[15] Some international human rights groups believe that the official count is much lower than the actual number. Amnesty International concluded that the number of executions was closer to 3,400 per year, and some international human rights organizations put the number as high as 10,000 or 15,000 a year, or around 30 to 40 a day, more than the rest of the world combined.

Dr. Wu Weihan was arrested in Beijing in 2005 and charged with conducting espionage for Taiwan. Wu, who had received his Ph.D. in Germany in the 1990s, worked in an Austrian biomedical company as a researcher at the time of his arrest. According to some rights organizations' sources, Wu was convicted in a closed trial. It was also reported that he was mistreated in detention and coerced into confession.[16] Dr. Wu was sentenced to death in May 2007 by a Beijing court. No appeal and no family visits were allowed by the court during his entire prison time. One day before his execution, the court gave special permission to his daughter's visit. On November 28, 2008, Wu was executed by gunshot.

The Supreme Court only regained the right to review all death penalty decisions on January 1, 2007. Even though a debate continues concerning the death sentence and criticism has increased within legal circles, there is no plan to abolish the practice.

In short, the extreme emphasis on punishment reflects China's legal tradition that the core purpose of law is to enforce punitive measures rather than to protect rights. This also reflects the traditional view that the state's authority to maintain social order, within which all people can benefit, should always be preserved. The extensive use of capital punishment clearly represents the government's intention to maintain political stability and social order. Guided by legal instrumentalism, the government has perpetuated the tradition that the nation's collective interests transcend individual rights.

NEED A LAWYER?

Defendants' rights have only recently become an indispensable part of the criminal justice system. On May 15, 1996, the National People's Congress passed new legislation to reform criminal justice procedures and the legal profession. The new system allows lawyers to establish their own private firms. China now recognizes that attorneys represent their clients, not the government, and that they can accept cases directly from defendants rather than through the government. Article 2 of the Lawyer's Law of the PRC defines attorneys as "professionals who have obtained a practicing license through legal means to provide legal services." Article 3 provides that practicing lawyers must follow the legal codes in the constitution and ethical codes in their professional discipline when they provide required legal aid and service.

During the legal reform in the second half of the 1990s, Chinese lawyers began to resume their legal service in lawsuits. In 1996, the NPC made it clear in its amendments of the 1979 Criminal Law that a suspect may maintain innocence before his or her conviction of a crime. According to the amendments, beginning in January 1997, suspects could hire a lawyer for their defense. Their lawyers can launch a limited investigation and argue their defendant's case in open court. Defense lawyers are still subject to critical restrictions when exercising this right, however. In terms of the temporary coercive measures used to detain people before they are formally charged, both legal codes and practices are lacking in the protection of rights and judicial measures. This is why, in 2004, China's criminal justice regime took especially serious efforts to curb the number of cases of unlawful lengthy detention of suspects.

Legal Aid

According to official sources, the establishment and development of the attorney and legal aid systems are playing "an increasingly important role in the protection of the legitimate rights and interests of citizens and the maintenance of legal enforcement of the law."[17] In 2000, China had nearly 9,500 law offices, including 92 foreign and 28 Hong Kong law firms, and the number of licensed lawyers exceeded 110,000.[18] That year, more than 310,000 criminal cases were defended by the lawyers, and over 170,000 cases received some kind of legal assistance at the procedural and investigative stages. Among these, over 228,000 received legal aid. In 2000, China had 1,853 legal assistance offices at various government levels and 6,109 full-time personnel, offering consultancy on law-related problems to 830,000 persons.[19]

By 2002, 2,418 legal aid offices operated throughout the country, and as public service agencies, provided aid to 129,775 individuals. In 2003, the Supreme Court formulated and promulgated the Regulations on Legal Aid. The high court developed a human network for the country's legal service system and defined a scale of citizens' rights to such services. By the end of that year, the number of offices had increased to 2,774 and served 166,433 cases. By 2007, China had 12,285 full-time legal aid personnel who provided legal services to 420,000 cases. In that year, China had more than 150,000 lawyers.

To practice, attorneys must first obtain professional qualifications. The 1996 Lawyer's Law provides for two approaches to meet the requirements. One way is to pass a national examination. As a second option, a person with a three-year college education in law can be granted, without taking the national test, a lawyer's qualifications after approval from judicial authorities. Once the initial qualification is obtained, lawyers need to apply for their license to practice. The local judicial authorities will form an opinion after they receive the application documents and report to the provincial judicial authorities. Those at the provincial, municipal, and autonomous regional level will grant or reject a practicing license to applicants. Attorneys must register their license annually. After passing these hurdles, lawyers may establish their own law firms. The 1996 legislation provided for three forms of law firms: state-funded, cooperative, and partnership.

Criminal Defense and Prisoners' Rights

In fact, it is difficult for ordinary Chinese citizens to receive legal aid and defend themselves. First of all, many lawyers work for the official jurisdictional system and perform a dual duty. Usually they tried to balance the case between the defendants' rights and the legal system, to which they partially belong. Defendant's rights have become negotiable in the criminal justice process. Some attorneys don't want to take on sensitive cases, and some of those who do defend political dissidents and complain about unfairness end up in jail themselves.

Second, there are still critical restrictions on defense lawyers. Their investigations are limited when they attempt to call defense witnesses and argue their client's case in court. An attorney often has difficulty meeting with the client or procurator, as well as obtaining necessary information to formulate a defense. The police and courts often use excuses such as a national security imperative to refuse to provide or share evidence with defense lawyers.

Third, the legal cost is an immense obstacle for most defendants to hire a lawyer who can actually defend them. Theoretically, if an accused is unable to hire a defender for economic reasons, the court may appoint a legal-aid attorney to defend the accused free of charge. Chapter 6 of the Lawyer's Law defines the scope of legal assistance and requires lawyers to provide it. However, since the funding comes from the government, the public lawyers in many cases will not defend the accused, especially in official corruption, government mismanagement, illegal land seizure, and unpaid wages cases.

For these reasons, the rights of many of the accused continue to be curtailed by law enforcement agencies. According to statistics from 2006, only 30 percent of all prisoners had a lawyer or legal consultant on their case. Defense attorneys face chronic difficulties in accessing information or clients. Among 933,156 defendants tried, only 1,147 were found not guilty.

China had a total of 1.8 million prisoners in jail in 2007, and the lack of protection for prisoners' rights has remained one of the major legal problems in the country. In 2003, the Ministry of Justice, based on the Law on Prisons, formulated and implemented the Regulations on Reform through Reeducation in Prisons, Regulations on the Procedures for Applications by Prisons for Commutation and Parole, and Regulations on Visits to and Correspondence of Foreign Prisoners. Meanwhile, the Ministry of Justice is continuing to try to reform the ways in which punishment in prisons is imposed and the management of prisons.

Safeguarding Lawyers

The role of lawyers in China is different than that of their counterparts in the United States, though the actual services rendered are very similar. Article 1 of the Lawyer's Law of the PRC provides that attorneys are "the state's legal workers." This makes it clear that the Chinese lawyer's first loyalty is to the state and its development. Those who do not serve the government's best interests risk losing their license and legal practice and can even face criminal charges. In November 2006, authorities cracked down on lawyers, and a number of top professionals and civil rights activists were arrested. On December 22, 2006, for example, the Beijing No. 1 Intermediate Court sentenced a lawyer to a three-year prison term for "inciting subversion of the national government" after he defended his client in court.

The trials and executions of Uyghurs charged with separatism continue—during 2003, the Chinese government stated that it had prosecuted more than 3,000 cases in Xinjiang—and the terrorism charges brought against them make it difficult for lawyers to represent the defendants.

From time to time, authorities also ignore the legal process and refuse to accept the lawyers' cases. For example, in Taishi village, Dongzhou, in the southern province of Guangdong, a standoff had arisen over property issues. The villagers rejected the government's offer of receiving a new power plant in exchange for surrendering their land. On December 7, 2005, thousands of villagers and their lawyers attempted to exercise their rights to appeal to the Dongzhou government. Officials reacted by sending in several hundred policemen who attacked the villagers, beating, arresting, and opening fire on them. Two villagers were shot to death and several dozen were wounded. The farmers were angry because they saw themselves as the weaker masses who did not have legal protection.

The decade of 1999–2009 was extraordinary important for the Chinese legal system. There was continuity and change, and a similar resilience can be predicted for the decade of 2010–2020. These changes in the legal system are very significant because they are signs of truly momentous changes in the political system for civil liberties and democracy. To continue the changes, as some of the international rights organizations suggest, the Chinese government must continue to reform the legal system "to conform to international standards." The Chinese government should "allow the petition and court systems to play a larger role in combating corruption at local levels, while providing free rein to the media, NGOs, and citizens to expose cases of corruption."[20] Adequate protection from officials must be ensured for petitioners, litigants, and whistle-blowers. The authorities must ensure the success of further political reform in China.

Notes

INTRODUCTION

1. Tania Branigan, "Barack Obama Meets Shanghai Students in China," Guardian.co.uk, November 16, 2009, http://www.guardian.co.uk/world/2009/nov/16/barack-obama-shanghai-students-china.

2. Benjamin I. Schwartz, *The World of Thought in Ancient China* (Cambridge, MA: Harvard University Press, 1985), chapters 3 and 8.

3. John K. Fairbank and Merle Goldman, *China: A New History*, enl. ed. (Cambridge, MA: Harvard University Press, 1998), 225–28.

4. Jonathan D. Spence, *The Search for Modern China*, 2nd ed. (New York: Norton, 1999), 257–58.

5. Xiaobing Li, *A History of the Modern Chinese Army* (Lexington: University Press of Kentucky, 2007), 31.

6. Richard Peters and Xiaobing Li, *Voices of the Korean War: Personal Stories of American, Korean, and Chinese Soldiers* (Lexington: University Press of Kentucky, 2004), 120.

7. Chen Jian and Xiaobing Li, "China and the End of the Cold War," in Malcolm Muir Jr., ed., *From Détente to the Soviet Collapse* (Lexington: Virginia Military Institute, 2006), 120.

8. Deng Xiaoping, "Emancipate the Mind, Seek Truth from Facts, and Unite as One in Looking to the Future," in *Selected Works of Deng Xiaoping* (Beijing: Foreign Languages Press, 1994), 2:150–63.

9. Ibid., 97.

CHAPTER 1

Portions of this chapter are reprinted from Xiaobing Li, "Military Modernization and Peaceful Rising: A Harmonious Transition of the PLA into the Future," *Peace and Conflict Studies* 16, No. 2 (Winter 2009), 17–32.

1. Mao Zedong, "On the People's Democratic Dictatorship," commemoration of the twenty-eighth anniversary of the CCP on June 30, 1949, in *Selected Works of Mao Tse-tung* (Beijing: Foreign Languages Press, 1977), 4:411–24.

2. In fact, the people's assessors system did not become formalized in the new republic until September 1951 when the Provisional Regulations for the Structure of People's Court Organization was stipulated.

3. Xiaobing Li, *A History of the Modern Chinese Army* (Lexington: University Press of Kentucky, 2007), 236–38.

4. S. C. Leng and H. Chiu, *Criminal Justice in Post-Mao China* (Albany: State University of New York Press, 1985), 78, 89.

5. Merle Goldman and Roderick MacFarquhar, "Dynamic Economy, Declining Party-State," in Merle Goldman and Roderick MacFarquhar, eds., *The Paradox of China's Post-Mao Reforms* (Cambridge, MA: Harvard University Press, 1999), 8.

6. Xiao Yang, "Zuigao Renmin Fayuan gongzuo baogao, 2007" (Supreme Court work report, 2007), March 14, 2007, available online at http://www.chinacourt.org/public/detail.php?id=239089.

7. Ministry of Justice, *Zhongguo falu nianjian, 1994–2005* (China law yearbook, 1994–2005) (Beijing: Law Press, 2006).

8. Chen Yanni, "Police Get New Rules on Use of Weapons," *China Daily*, January 30, 1996.

9. Weixing Chen, "Economic Reform and Social Instability in Rural China," in Jie Zhang and Xiaobing Li, eds., *Social Transition in China* (Lanham, MD: University Press of America, 1998), 96–97.

10. According to figures in the *People's Armed Police News* (Beijing) in 1997 and 2000.

11. Xinhua News Agency, "Law of the People's Republic of China on National Defense, Adopted at the Fifth Session of the Eighth National People's Congress, March 14, 1997," Foreign Broadcast Information Service (FBIS) CHI-97-255.

12. Ibid.

13. Jiafang Chen, "Crime in China's Modernization," in Zhang and Li, *Social Transition in China*, 158.

14. All of the mentioned documents can be found in *White Papers of the Chinese Government, 1996–1999*, comp. Information Office of the PRC State Council (Beijing: Foreign Languages Press, 2000).

15. *White Papers of China's National Defense in 2004*, comp. Information Office of the PRC State Council (Beijing: Foreign Languages Press, 2005), 654.

16. Li, *A History of the Modern Chinese Army*, 292–93.

CHAPTER 2

1. An English translation of the 1982 Constitution and its amendments is available in Standing Committee of the National People's Congress, *The Constitution of the People's Republic of China* (Beijing: People's Publishing House, 2004).

2. "Progress in China's Human Rights Cause in 2003," in *White Papers of the Chinese Government*, comp. Information Office of the PRC State Council (Beijing: Foreign Languages Press, 2005), 4:401.

3. Ibid., 4:410.

4. Ibid., 4:400.

5. Xiaobing Li, "Social–Economic Transition and Cultural Reconstruction in China," in Zhang and Li, eds., *Social Transition in China* (Lanham, MD: University Press of America, 1998), 10–11.

6. Articles 90 and 102 of the Criminal Law.

7. "Chinese Author in Freedom of Speech Drama," Radio Free Asia report, available online at http://rfa.org/englilsh/news/china_author-20070205.html.

8. "China to Release Aging Opposition Activist Ahead of U.S. Trip," Radio Free Asia report, available online at http://www.rfa.org/englilsh/news/china_dissident-20060308.html.

9. As the founding father of the Republic of China and the Guomindang, Sun Zhongshan mobilized the masses for the 1911 Republican Revolution with his Three Principles of the People: nationalism (both anti-Manchu and anti-imperialist), democracy (a constitution with people's rights), and "people's livelihood" (a classic term for social equality). For more details, see the introduction.

10. Kelly Sanja, Christopher Walker, and Jake Dizard, eds., *Countries at the Crossroads: A Survey of Democratic Governance, 2007* (New York: Rowman & Littlefield, 2008), 173.

11. Human Rights Watch, "China: Legal Reforms," in *World Report: 2008* (New York: Human Rights Watch, 2008), 262.

CHAPTER 3

1. Information Office of the PRC State Council, "Freedom of Religious Belief in China," October 1997, in *White Papers of the Chinese Government*, comp. Information Office of the PRC State Council (Beijing: Foreign Languages Press, 2005), 2:241, available online at http://china-tesol.com/Religion_1/Religious_Freedom/religious_freedom.html.

2. "Chinese Christian Dies in Police Custody, Others Detained," Radio Free Asia report, available online at http://www.rfa.org/englilsh/news/politics/137033-20040531.html.

3. "Regional Ethnic Autonomy in Tibet," May 2004, in *White Papers of the Chinese Government*, 4:529–30.

4. "History and Development of Xinjiang," May 2003, in *White Papers of the Chinese Government*, 4:278–79.

5. Human Rights Watch, "China: Events of 2007," in *World Report: 2008* (New York: Human Rights Watch, 2008), available online at http://www.hrw.org/legacy/englishwr2k8/docs/2008/01/31/china17604.htm.

6. "China Tells Living Buddhas to Obtain Permission before They Reincarnate." http://www.takungpao.com/news/06/03/21/ZM.

7. "Faith without Freedom," Radio Free Asia report, available online at http://www.rfa.org/englilsh/vietnam/asia_pope-20050408.html.

8. Kelly Sanja, Christopher Walker, and Jake Dizard, eds., *Countries at the Crossroads: A Survey of Democratic Governance, 2007* (New York: Rowman & Littlefield, 2008), 176–77.

9. Interview with Li Hongzhi, *Time*, May 10, 1999, available online at http://www.time.com/asia/magazine/1999/990510/interview1.html.

10. "The Appalling State of Human Rights in China," *Chasing Evil*, July 1, 2008, http://www.chasingevil.org/2008/07/china.html.

11. Falun Dafa Information Center, "Overview of Persecution," May 4, 2008, http://www.faluninfo.net/topic/2/.

12. In 1951, the Chinese government and Tibet signed the Agreement on Measures for the Peaceful Liberation of Tibet. The agreement affirmed Tibet's political, social, and religious autonomy. In 1959, however, the Chinese government accused the Dalai Lama of organizing a separatist movement in Tibet. PLA troops suppressed the rebellion and the Dalai Lama escaped into India. For more details, see Li, *A History of the Modern Chinese Army* (Lexington: University Press of Kentucky, 2007), 198–99.

13. Human Rights Watch, "China: Events of 2007."

14. Ibid., 269.

15. "Xinjiang to Speed Up Legislation against Separatism, Regional Top Lawmaker," Xinhua, July 20, 2009, available online at http://news.

xinhuanet.com/English/2009-07/20/content_11734279.htm. See also "After Riots, China to Promote Anti-Separatist Laws," ABC News, July 20, 2009, available online at http://abcnews.go.com/International/wireStory?id=8123676.

16. Thomas Gold, "China," in Sanja, Walker, and Dizard, *Countries at the Crossroads*, 1–35, available online at http://www.freedomhouse.org/uploads/ccr/country-7155-8.pdf.

CHAPTER 4

1. China Internet Information Center, "White Paper on Human Rights Published," March 30, 2004, http://www.china.org.cn/english/2004/Mar/91638.htm.

2. China Internet Information Center, "China to Reinforce Government Spokesperson System," November 8, 2003, http://www.china.org.cn/english/government/79595.htm.

3. "Progress in China's Human Rights Cause in 2003," in *White Papers of the Chinese Government*, comp. Information Office of the PRC State Council (Beijing: Foreign Languages Press, 2005), 4:408.

4. Phelim Kine, "A Gold Medal in Media Censorship," in Minky Worden, ed., *China's Great Leap: The Beijing Games and Olympian Human Rights Challenges* (New York: Seven Stories Press, 2008), 117–18.

5. *Zhongguo Qingnianbao* (*China Youth Daily*), January 14, 2002.

6. Human Rights in China, "Independent Report by Human Rights Group in China, August 23, 2002, available online at http://www.hrichina.org.

7. "Former Top Chinese Aide in Warning over Press Freedom," Radio Free Asia report, February 14, 2007, available online at http://www.rfa.org/english/china/china_baotong-20070214.html.

8. Joseph Amon, "High Hurdles to Health in China," in Minky Worden, ed., *China's Great Leap,* 133–38.

9. U.S. Congress, Congressional-Executive Commission on China, "Political Prisoner Database," in *Annual Report, 2006*, 118–19, available online at http://www.cecc.gov/pages/annualRpt/annualRpt06/PoliticalPrisonerDatabase.php.

10. For more details of the Shi Tao case, see Thomas Gold, "China," in Kelly Sanja, Christopher Walker, and Jake Dizard, eds., *Countries at the Crossroads: A Survey of Democratic Governance, 2007* (New York: Rowman & Littlefield, 2008), 8, available online at http://www.freedomhouse.org/uploads/ccr/country-7155-8.pdf and http://www.amnestyusa.org/business/Undermining_Freedom_of_Expression_in_China.pdf.

11. Human Rights Watch, "Summary of China Rights Developments," n.d., http://china.hrw.org/press/review/summary_of_china_rights_developments

12. For more details, see "U.S. Human Rights Report: China," *Journal of Turkish Weekly*, February 25, 2009, http://www.turkishweekly.net/news/65500.

13. Miguel Helft, "Google Hopes to Retain Business Unit in China," *New York Times*, January 19, 2010.

14. Sharon LaFraniere, "China to Scan Text Messages to Spot 'Unhealthy Content,'" *New York Times*, January 19, 2010.

CHAPTER 5

1. The Gini coefficient is an internationally accepted statistical system to measure the inequality of income and wealth distributions. It is a ratio with values between 0 and 1. A low Gini coefficient indicates more equal income or wealth distribution; a high Gini coefficient indicates greater inequity. By comparison, the Gini coefficients were 0.232 for Denmark and 0.428 for the United States in 2000.

2. Li Xiaoxiao and Zhou Mei, "A Comparative Study on Minority Women in Taiwan and Xinjiang," in Xiaobing Li and Zuohong Pan, eds., *Taiwan in the Twenty-First Century* (New York: University Press of America, 2003), 83–96.

3. Xiaobing Li, "The Impact of Social Changes on the PLA: A Chinese Military Perspective," in David M. Finkelstein and Kristen Gunness, eds., *Civil-Military Relations in Today's China: Swimming in a New Sea* (Armonk, NY: M. E. Sharpe, 2007), 41–42.

4. U.S. Department of State, Bureau of Democracy, Human Rights, and Labor, "China," 2005 annual report, March 8, 2006, available online at http://www.state.gov/g/drl/rls/hrrpt/2005/61605.htm.

5. "World Federation of the Trade Unions Discovers the Workers Abuse in China's Factories," *Newsletters of the Chinese Labors*, November 20, 2006, available online (in Chinese) at http://big5.china-labour.org.hk/public/contents/news?revision%5fid=101243. Available online (in English) at http://big5.china-labour.org.hk.

6. The detailed report is available at Human Rights Watch, "Summary of China Rights Developments," n.d., http://china.hrw.org/press/review/summary_of_china_rights_developments.

7. Taiwan Foundation for Democracy, *China Human Rights Report 2007* (Taibei, Taiwan: Taiwan Foundation for Democracy, 2008), 25.

8. "Fifty Years of Progress in China's Human Rights," in *White Papers of the Chinese Government*, comp. Information Office of the PRC State Council (Beijing: Foreign Languages Press, 2003), 3:89.

9. Human Rights Group, "The 2003 Annual Report on the Rights and Interests of Women and Children, March 31, 2004," available at

http://www.humanrights.cn and Information Office of the PRC State Council, *White Papers of the Chinese Government* (Beijing: Foreign Languages Press, 2005), 421–22.

10. UK Border Agency, Country of Origin Information Service, *China*, April 16, 2009, available online at http://www.unhcr.org/refworld/pdfid/49e86e772.pdf.

11. U.S. Department of State, Bureau of Democracy, Human Rights, and Labor, "2008 Human Rights Report: China," February 25, 2009, available online at http://www.state.gov/g/drl/rls/hrrpt/2008/eap/119037.htm.

12. Human Rights Watch, *World Report 2007* (New York: Human Rights Watch, 2008), 265–66.

13. "Progress in China's Human Rights Cause in 2003," in *White Papers of the Chinese Government* (2005), 4:421.

14. For details of Chen's kidnapping, see "Blind Chinese Activist Describes 38-Hour Kidnapping by Shandong Officials," Radio Free Asia report, September 8, 2005, available online at http://www.rfa.org/english/news/china_kidnapping-20050908.html.

15. Xinhua News Agency, "China Vows to Halt Growing Gender Imbalance," January 23, 2007, http://English.people.com.cn/200701/23/eng20070123_343739.html.

16. Taiwan Foundation for Democracy, *China Human Rights 2008* (Taibei, Taiwan: Taiwan Foundation for Democracy, 2009), 12–13.

17. Thomas Gold, "China," in Kelly Sanja, Christopher Walker, and Jake Dizard, eds., *Countries at the Crossroads: A Survey of Democratic Governance, 2007* (New York: Rowman & Littlefield, 2008), available online at http://www.freedomhouse.org/uploads/ccr/country-7155-8.pdf.

CHAPTER 6

Portions of this chapter are reprinted from Xiaobing Li, "Military Modernization and Peaceful Rising: A Harmonious Transition of the PLA into the Future," *Peace and Conflict Studies* 16, No. 2 (Winter 2009), 17–32.

1. Human Rights Watch, "China: Events of 2007," in *World Report: 2008* (New York: Human Rights Watch, 2008), available online at http://hrw.org/legacy/englilshwr2k8/docs/2008/01/31/china17604.htm.

2. Ibid., 5.

3. U.S. Department of State, Bureau of Democracy, Human Rights, and Labor, "China," 2006 annual report, March 6, 2007, available online at http://www.state.gov/g/drl/rls/hrrpt/2006/78771.htm.

4. Supreme People's Court, *Quanguo Fayuan Shenli Zhixing Anjian Qingkuang* (Annual reports: Details of cases tried and enforced nationwide), available online (in Chinese) at http://www.dffy.com/sifashijian/ziliao/20070314163527.htm.

5. Ibid.

6. Xinhua News Agency, "The Overall Quality of Our Nation's Judges and Procurators," *Renmin Ribao* (People's daily), July 17, 2005, available online at http://news.xinhuanet.com/legal/2005-07/17/content_3228617.htm.

7. Supreme People's Court, "Zengqiang Sifa Nengli Tigao Sifa Shuiping de Yijian, 2005" (Instructions on improving judicial quality and efficiency, 2005), in Supreme People's Court, ed., *Zhongguo Changyong Sifa Jieshi Quanshu* (Complete law and interpretations of the PRC) (Beijing: Minzhu Fazhi Press, 2007), 6–89.

8. Information Office of the PRC's State Council, "Progress in China's Human Rights Cause in 1996," in Information Office of the PRC's State Council, ed., *White Papers of the Chinese Government, 1996–1999* (Beijing: Foreign Languages Press, 2000), 178.

9. Human Rights Watch, *World Report 2008* (New York: Human Rights Watch, 2009), 264.

10. Gao Zhehan et al., *Zhongguo Wujing da Jiegou* (The Inside Stories of the Chinese People's Armed Police) (Taibei, Taiwan: Yangzhi Cultural Press, 2003), 180–81.

11. For more details on the Paltsal Kyab case, see the report available at http://www.de-sci.org/blogs/tecel/category/%E8%BD%AC%E8%BD%BD/ or Amnesty International, "Amnesty International Testimony Human Rights in China before Human Rights Commission Committee on Foreign Affairs United States Congress," available at http://www.amnestyusa.ord/document.php?id=ENGUSA20090127008&lang=e.

12. Thomas Gold, "China," in Kelly Sanja, Christopher Walker, and Jake Dizard, eds., *Countries at the Crossroads: A Survey of Democratic Governance, 2007* (New York: Rowman & Littlefield, 2008), available online at http://www.freedomhouse.org/uploads/ccr/country-7155-8.pdf.

13. "Progress in China's Human Rights Cause in 2003," in *White Papers of the Chinese Government*, comp. Information Office of the PRC State Council (Beijing: Foreign Languages Press, 2005), 4:413.

14. U.S. Department of State, "China."

15. "China, Iran Lead in Executions in 2005," Radio Free Europe/Radio Liberty report, April 20, 2006, available online at http://www.rferl.org/featuresarticle/2006/04/e9e4f63e-6ff6-43ef-8468-14af5b2e86ac.html.

16. For more details on the Wu Weihan case, see reports available at http://www.de-sci.org/blogs/tecel/category/%E8%BD%AC%E8%BD%BD/ or Amnesty International, "Amnesty International Testimony Human Rights in China before Human Rights Commission Committee on Foreign Affairs United States Congress," available at http://www.amnestyusa.ord/document.php?id=ENGUSA20090127008&lang=e.

17. Information Office of the PRC's State Council, "Progress in China's Human Rights Cause in 2000," in Information Office of the PRC's State Council, ed., *White Papers of the Chinese Government, 2000–2001* (Beijing: Foreign Languages Press, 2002), 397.

18. The official statistics are available online at http://www.chinagate.cn/English/1719.htm. See also Information Office of the PRC State Council, "Progress in China's Human Rights Cause in 2000," in Information Office of the PRC State Council, *White Papers of the Chinese Government, 2000–2001* (Beijing: Foreign Languages Press, 2002), 396–97.

19. "Progress in China's Human Rights Cause in 2000," April 2001, in *White Papers of the Chinese Government* (2003), 3:397–98.

20. Sophie Richardson, "Challenges for a 'Responsible Power'," in Human Rights Watch, *World Report 2008* (New York: Human Rights Watch, 2009), 33–34.

Selected Bibliography

BOOKS

All-China Federation of Trade Unions Policy Research Office. *Chinese Trade Unions Statistics Yearbook*. Beijing: Labor Press, 2000.

Amnesty International. *Political Imprisonment in the People's Republic of China*. London: Amnesty International, 1978.

Bailey, Paul J. *China in the Twentieth Century*. 2nd ed. Malden, MA: Blackwell, 2001.

Barme, Geremie R. *In the Red: On Contemporary Chinese Culture*. New York: Columbia University Press, 1999.

Baum, Richard. *Burying Mao: Chinese Politics in the Age of Deng Xiaoping*. Princeton, NJ: Princeton University Press, 1994.

Bodde, Derek, and Clarence Morris. *Law in Imperial China*. Philadelphia: Pennsylvania University Press, 1973.

Cambridge History of China. Vol. 14, *The People's Republic*. Cambridge, UK: University of Cambridge Press, 1967.

Chang, Gordon. *The Coming Collapse of China*. New York: Random House, 2001.

Chang, Jung, and Jon Halliday. *Mao: The Unknown Story*. New York: Knopf, 2005.

Chang, Wei Jen. *Traditional Chinese and Attitudes toward Law and Authority*. Hong Kong: Centre for Contemporary Asian Studies, Chinese University of Hong Kong, 1986.

Chen, Jiafang. "Crime in China's Modernization." In *Social Transition in China*, ed. Jie Zhang and Xiaobing Li. Lanham, MD: University Press of America, 1998.

Chen, Jian, and Xiaobing Li. "China and the End of the Cold War." In *From Détente to the Soviet Collapse*, ed. Malcolm Muir Jr. Lexington: Virginia Military Institute, 2006.

China. Information Office of the PRC State Council. *Progress in China's Human Rights Cause in 1996*. Beijing: Information Office of the PRC State Council, 1997.

China. *White Papers of the Chinese Government, 1996–1999*. Beijing: Foreign Languages Press, 2000.

China. Ministry of Justice. *The Criminal Procedure Law of China*. Beijing: Foreign Languages Press, 1984.

China. *Zhongguo Falu Nianjian, 1985–2005* (Law yearbook of China, 1985–2005). Beijing: China Law Press, 1987–2007.

China. Standing Committee of the National People's Congress. *The Constitution of the People's Republic of China*. Beijing: People's Publishing House, 2004.

China. State Family Planning Commission. *Population and Family Planning Law*. Beijing: NPC Press, 2002.

China. Supreme People's Court. *Quanguo Fayuan Shenli Zhixing Anjian Qingkuang* (Annual reports: Details of cases tried and enforced nationwide). Available online (in Chinese) at http://www.dffy.com/sifashijian/ziliao/20070314163527.htm.

China. Supreme People's Court. "Zengqiang Sifa Nengli Tigao Sifa Shuiping de Yijian, 2005" (Instructions on improving judicial quality and efficiency, 2005). In *Zhongguo Changyong Sifa Jieshi Quanshu* (Complete law and interpretations of the PRC). Beijing: Democracy and Law Press, 2007.

China Internet Network Information Center. *Survey Report on Internet Development in China*. Beijing: CNNIC, 2003.

Cohen, J. A. *The Criminal Process in the People's Republic of China: An Introduction*. Cambridge, MA: Harvard University Press, 1968.

Cohen, Warren I. *America's Response to China: A History of Sino-American Relations*. 4th ed. New York: Columbia University Press, 2000.

Collection of PRC Law. Constitutional Law. Beijing: People's Press, 1985.

Commercial, Business and Trade Laws of the PRC. New York: Oceana, 1985.

Conboy, Kenneth, and James Morrison. *The CIA's Secret War in Tibet*. Lawrence: University Press of Kansas, 2002.

Croll, Elizabeth. *Changing Identities of Chinese Women*. Hong Kong: Hong Kong University Press, 1995.

Croll, Elizabeth, Deborah Davis, and Penny Kane, eds. *China's One-Child Policy.* London: Macmillan, 1985.

Dalai Lama. *Freedom in Exile: The Autobiography of the Dalai Lama.* San Francisco: HarperCollins, 1991.

Deng, Xiaoping. *Selected Works of Deng Xiaoping.* Beijing: Foreign Languages Press, 1994.

Economy, Elizabeth, and Michel Oksenberg, eds. *China Joins the World: Progress and Prospects.* New York: Council on Foreign Relations Press, 1999.

Editorial Board for Law Teaching Materials. *Constitutional Law.* Beijing: Mass Press, 1984.

Editorial Board for Law Teaching Materials. *General Principles of Law.* Beijing: Law Press, 1984.

Editorial Board for Law Teaching Materials. *Principles of Administrative Law.* Beijing: Law Press, 1983.

Edwards, R. R., L. Henkin, and Andrew J. Nathan. *Human Rights in Contemporary China.* New York: Columbia University Press, 1968.

Fairbank, K. John, and Merle Goldman. *China: A New History.* Enl. ed. Cambridge, MA: Harvard University Press, 1998.

Fei Hsiao Tung. *Chinese Village Close-up.* Beijing: New World Press, 1983.

Feng, Peter. *Intellectual Property in China.* Hong Kong: Sweet & Maxwell Asia, 1997.

Feng, Tongqing. *The Fate of Chinese Labor: Labor's Social Actions since the Reform.* Beijing: Social Science Documents Press, 2002.

Finkelstein, David M., and Kristen Gunness, eds. *Civil-Military Relations in Today's China: Swimming in a New Sea.* Armonk, NY: M. E. Sharpe, 2006.

Freedom House. *Countries at the Crossroads.* New York: Freedom House, 2004.

Freedom House. *The Worst of the Worst: The World's Most Repressive Societies, 2008.* Washington, DC: Freedom House, 2008.

Gearty, C. A. *Essays on Human Rights and Terrorism: Comparative Approaches to Civil Liberties in Asia, the EU and North America.* London: Cameron May, 2008.

Gernet, Jacques. *China and the Christian Impact: A Conflict of Cultures.* Cambridge, UK: Cambridge University Press, 1990.

Goldman, Merle. *Sowing the Seeds of Democracy in China.* Cambridge, MA: Harvard University Press, 1999.

Goldman, Merle, and Roderick MacFarquhar, eds. *The Paradox of China's Post-Mao Reforms.* Cambridge, MA: Harvard University Press, 1999.

Goldstein, Jonathan, ed. *The Jews in China.* Armonk, NY: M. E. Sharpe, 2000.

Goldstein, Melvyn C., Dawei Sherap, and William R. Siebenschuh. *A Tibetan Revolutionary.* Berkeley: University of California Press, 2004.

Goodman, David S. G., and Gerald Segal, eds. *China in the Nineties: Crisis Management and Beyond*. Oxford, UK: Oxford University Press, 1991.

Grasso, June, Jay Corrin, and Michael Kort. *Modernization and Revolution in China: From the Opium Wars to World Power*. 3rd ed. Armonk, NY: M. E. Sharpe, 2004.

Gries, Peter Hays. *China's New Nationalism: Pride, Politics, and Diplomacy*. Berkeley: University of California Press, 2004.

Guttentag, Marcia, and Paul F. Secord. *Too Many Women? The Sex Ratio Question*. Thousand Oaks, CA: Sage, 1983.

Hamrin, Carol Lee, and Timothy Cheek, eds. *China's Establishment Intellectuals*. Armonk, NY: M. E. Sharpe, 2004.

Hao, Zhidong. *Intellectuals at a Crossroads: The Changing Politics of China's Knowledge Workers*. Albany: State University of New York Press, 2003.

Harding, Harry. *A Fragile Relationship: The United States and China since 1972*. Washington, DC: Brookings Institution, 1992.

He, Zhou, and Huailin Chen. *The Chinese Media: A New Perspective*. Hong Kong: Pacific Century Press, 2002.

Hong, Junhao. *The Internationalization of Television in China: The Evolution of Ideology, Society, and Media since the Reform*. Westport, CT: Praeger, 1998.

Hook, Brian, ed. *The Individual and the State in China*. New York: Clarendon Press, 1996.

Hsiung, James C., ed. *Hong Kong, the Super Paradox: Life after Return to China*. New York: St. Martin's Press, 2000.

Human Rights Watch. "China: Legal Reforms." In *World Report, 2008*. New York: Human Rights Watch, 2008.

Hutchings, Graham. *Modern China: A Guide to a Century of Change*. Cambridge, MA: Harvard University Press, 2001.

Kent, Ann. *China, the United Nations, and Human Rights: The Limits of Compliance*. Philadelphia: University of Pennsylvania Press, 1999.

Kim, Samuel S. *China, the United Nations, and World Order*. Princeton, NJ: Princeton University Press, 1979.

Kine, Phelim. "A Gold Medal in Media Censorship." In *China's Great Leap: The Beijing Games and Olympian Human Rights Challenges*, ed. Minky Worden. New York: Seven Stories Press, 2008.

Koeltl, John. *Civil Rights and Liberties in China*. Albany, NY: Albany Law School, 1982.

Kristof, Nicholas, and Sheryl Wudunn. *China Wakes: The Struggle for the Soul of a Rising Power*. New York: Vintage Books, 1994.

Lam, Willy Wo-Lap. *The Era of Jiang Zemin*. Singapore: Prentice-Hall, 1999.

Lan, Quanpu. *Developments in Chinese Law in the Last Thirty Years.* Beijing: People's Press, 1980.

Legal Teaching and Research Unit of the CCP Central Party School. *Basic Principles of Law.* Beijing: Central Party Academy Press, 1984.

Leng, S. C., and H. Chiu. *Criminal Justice in Post-Mao China.* Albany: State University of New York Press, 1985.

Levine, Marvin J. *Worker Rights and Labor Standards in Asia: A Comparative Perspective.* New York: Plenum Press, 1997.

Li, Cheng. *China's Leaders: The New Generation.* Lanham, MD: Rowman & Littlefield, 2001.

Li, Xiaobing. *A History of the Modern Chinese Army.* Lexington: University Press of Kentucky, 2007.

Lipman, Jonathan N. *Familiar Strangers: A History of Muslims in Northwest China.* Seattle: University of Washington Press, 1997.

Liu, Wenhua, and Ma Te. *Circumvention of the Conflict between the WTO and the Labor Legal System of China.* Beijing: China City Press, 2001.

Lynch, D. *After the Propaganda State: Media, Politics, and "Thought Work" in Reform China.* Stanford, CA: Stanford University Press, 1999.

Mackerras, Colin, and Amanda York. *The Cambridge Handbook of Contemporary China.* Cambridge, UK: Cambridge University Press, 1991.

Mao Zedong. *Selected Works of Mao Tse-tung.* Beijing: Foreign Languages Press, 1977.

Markoff, John. *Waves of Democracy: Social Movement and Political Change.* Thousand Oaks, CA: Pine Forge Press, 1996.

Meiklejohn Civil Liberties Institute. *Beijing Women's Conference: United States Government Official Comments and Report from the White House.* Berkeley, CA: Meiklejohn Civil Liberties Institute, 1995.

Meisner, Maurice. *Mao's China and After.* 3rd ed. New York: Free Press, 1999.

Nathan, Andrew J. *Chinese Democracy.* New York: Alfred A. Knopf, 1985.

Naughton, Barry. *The Chinese Economy: Transitions and Growth.* Boston: MIT Press, 2007.

Peters, Richard, and Xiaobing Li. *Voices of the Korean War: Personal Stories of American, Korean, and Chinese Soldiers.* Lexington: University Press of Kentucky, 2004.

Potter, Sulamith H., and Jack M. Potter. *China's Peasants: The Anthropology of a Revolution.* Cambridge, UK: Cambridge University Press, 1990.

Ren, Xiao. *China's Administrative Reform.* Zhejiang, China: Zhejiang People's Press, 1998.

Ren, Yanli, ed. *Basic Knowledge of Chinese Catholicism.* Beijing: Religious Culture Press, 2000.

Sanja, Kelly, Christopher Walker, and Jake Dizard, eds. *Countries at the Crossroads: A Survey of Democratic Governance, 2007*. New York: Rowman & Littlefield, 2008.

Schacht, Chris. *Report of the Australian Human Rights Delegation to China, 14–26 July 1991*. Canberra: Australian Government Publishing Service, 1991.

Schell, Orville, and David Shambaugh, eds. *The China Reader: The Reform Era*. New York: Vintage Books, 1999.

Schoppa, R. Keith. *Revolution and Its Past: Identities and Change in Modern Chinese History*. 2nd ed. Upper Saddle River, NJ: Prentice-Hall, 2006.

Schwartz, I. Benjamin. *The World of Thought in Ancient China*. Cambridge, MA: Harvard University Press, 1985.

Shambaugh, David. *Modernizing China's Military: Progress, Problems, and Prospects*. Berkeley: University of California Press, 2002.

Shapiro, J., and Liang Heng. *Cold Winds, Warm Winds: Intellectual Life in China Today*. Middletown, CT: Wesleyan University Press, 1986.

Shirk, Susan. *China: Fragile Superpower, How China's Internal Politics Could Derail Its Peaceful Rise*. New York: Oxford University Press, 2007.

Sieghart, P. *The International Law of Human Rights*. Oxford, UK: Clarendon Press, 1983.

Situ, Yingyi, and Weizheng Liu. "The Criminal Justice System of China." In *Comparative and International Criminal Justice Systems*, ed. Obi N. Ibnatius Ebbe. 2nd ed. Boston: Butterworth-Heinemann, 2000.

Spence, D. Jonathan. *The Search for Modern China*. 2nd ed. New York: Norton, 1999.

Terrill, J. Richard. *World Criminal Justice Systems: A Survey*. 4th ed. Cincinnati, OH: Anderson, 1999.

Tien, Hung-Mao, and Yun-han Chu, eds. *China under Jiang Zemin*. Boulder, CO: Lynne Rienner, 2000.

Turner, Karen G., James V. Feinerman, and R. Kent Guy. *The Limits of the Rule of Law in China*. Seattle: University of Washington Press, 2000.

U.S. Bureau of the Census. *1990 Census of Population and Housing*. Washington, DC: GPO, 1993.

U.S. Department of State. Bureau of Democracy, Human Rights, and Labor. "China." In *Country Reports on Human Rights Practices, 2006*. Washington, DC: GPO, 2007. Available online at http://www.state.gov/ g/drl/rls/hrrpt/2006/78771.htm.

Wacks, Raymond, and Wenmin Chen. *Civil Liberties in Hong Kong*. New York: Oxford University Press, 1988.

Wang, Fei-ling. *China's Hukou System: Organization through Division and Exclusion*. Stanford, CA: Stanford University Press, 2004.

Wang, J. C. F. *Contemporary Chinese Politics: An Introduction.* Englewood Cliffs, NJ: Prentice-Hall, 1980.

Wang, Kui Hua. *Chinese Commercial Law.* Oxford, UK: Oxford University Press, 2000.

Wang, Xiaoming. *Research on Certain Theoretical Questions Relating to the Constitution.* Beijing: Chinese People's University Press, 1983.

Warner, M. *The Management of Human Resources in Chinese Industry.* New York: St. Martin's Press, 1995.

Weng, Byron, ed. *Essays on the Constitution of the People's Republic of China.* Hong Kong: Chinese University Press, 1984.

Xin, Meng. *Labor Market Reform in China.* Cambridge, UK: Cambridge University Press, 2000.

Zhang, Jie, and Xiaobing Li, eds. *Social Transition in China.* New York: University Press of America, 1998.

Zhao, Yuezhi. *Media, Market, and Democracy in China: Between the Party Line and the Bottom Line.* Urbana: University of Illinois Press, 1998.

Zhehan, Gao et al. *Zhongguo Wujing da Jiegou (The Inside Stories of the Chinese People's Armed Police).* Taibei, Taiwan: Yangzhi Cultural Press, 2003.

Zhou, Kate Xiao. *How the Farmers Changed China: Power of the People.* Boulder, CO: Westview Press, 1996.

Zweig, David. *Internationalizing China: Domestic Interests and Global Linkages.* Ithaca, NY: Cornell University Press, 2002.

ARTICLES AND PAPERS

China. Information Office of the PRC State Council. "Fifty Years of Progress in China's Human Rights." In *White Papers of the Chinese Government* (Beijing: Foreign Languages Press, 2003).

China. Information Office of the PRC State Council. "Freedom of Religious Belief in China." October 1997. In *White Papers of the Chinese Government* (Beijing: Foreign Languages Press, 2005).

China. Information Office of the PRC State Council. "History and Development of Xinjiang." May 2003. In *White Papers of the Chinese Government* (Beijing: Foreign Languages Press, 2005).

———. "Labor and Social Security in China." In *White Papers of the Chinese Government* (Beijing: Foreign Languages Press, 2002).

China. Information Office of the PRC State Council. "Progress in China's Human Rights Cause in 2003." In *White Papers of the Chinese Government* (Beijing: Foreign Languages Press, 2005).

China. Information Office of the PRC State Council. "Regional Ethnic Autonomy in Tibet." May 2004. In *White Papers of the Chinese Government* (Beijing: Foreign Languages Press, 2005).

China Internet Information Center. "China to Reinforce Government Spokesperson System." November 8, 2003. Http://www.china.org.cn/english/government/79595.htm.

Hasan, Nader. "China's Forgotten Dissenters: The Long Fuse of Xinjiang." *Harvard International Review* 22, no. 3 (Fall 2000), 38–41.

Liu, Dimon. "Human Rights as the Basis for the Rule of Law." *China Strategic Review* 2, no. 6 (November/December 1997), 11–29.

Radio Free Asia. "China to Release Aging Opposition Activist Ahead of U.S. Trip." Available online at http://www.rfa.org/english/news/china_dissident-20060308.html.

Radio Free Asia. "Chinese Author in Freedom of Speech Drama." Available online at http://rfa.org/english/news/china_author-20070205.html.

Radio Free Asia. "Chinese Christian Dies in Police Custody, Others Detained." Available online at http://www.rfa.org/english/news/politics/137033-20040531.html.

Radio Free Asia. "Faith without Freedom." Available online at http://www.rfa.org/english/vietnam/asia_pope-20050408.html.

Radio Free Asia. "Former Top Chinese Aide in Warning over Press Freedom." Available online at http://www.rfa.org/english/china/china_baotong-20070214.html.

Radio Free Europe/Radio Liberty. "China, Iran Lead in Executions in 2005." April 20, 2006. Available online at http://www.rferl.org/featuresarticle/2006/04/e9e4f63e-6ff6-43ef-8468-14af5b2e86ac.html.

U.S. Congress. Congressional-Executive Commission on China. "Political Prisoner Database." In *Annual Report, 2006*, 118–19, available online at http://www.cecc.gov/pages/annualRpt/annualRpt06/PoliticalPrisonerDatabase.php

"World Federation of the Trade Unions Discovers the Workers Abuse in China's Factories." *Newsletters of the Chinese Labors.* November 20, 2006. Available online (in Chinese) at http://big5.china-labour.org.hk/public/contents/news?revision%5fid=101243. Available online (in English) at http://big5.china-labour.org.hk.

Xinhua News Agency. "China Vows to Halt Growing Gender Imbalance." January 23, 2007. Available online at http://English.people.com.cn/200701/23/eng20070123_343739.html.

Xinhua News Agency. "Law of the People's Republic of China on National Defense, Adopted at the Fifth Session of the Eighth National People's Congress on March 14, 1997." Foreign Broadcast Information Service, FBIS-CHI-97-255.

Xinhua News Agency. "The Overall Quality of Our Nation's Judges and Procurators." *Renmin Ribao* (People's Daily), July 17, 2005. Available online at http://news.xinhuanet.com/legal/2005-07/17/content_3228617.htm.

Yang, Xiao. "Zuigao Renmin Fayuan Gongzuo Baogao, 2007" (Supreme Court work report, 2007). March 14, 2007. Available online at http://www.chinacourt.org/public/detail.php?id=239089.

Yue, Yang, and Nanxiang Gong. "Between Tradition and Modernity: Civil Liberties in China." *China Strategic Review* 2, no. 4 (July/August 1997), 24–37.

WEBSITES

ActionAid China. www.actionaid.org/china

Amnesty International. www.amnesty.org

Asian Human Rights Commission. www.ahrchk.net/index.php

Asian Migrant Center (AMC). www.asian-migrants.org

Asian Monitor Resource Center (AMRC). www.amrc.org.hk

Beijing Spring (monthly magazine). http://bjzc.org

Business and Human Rights Resource Center (BHRRC). www.business-humanrights.org

Child Workers in Asia (CWA). www.cwa.tnet.co.th

China Aid Association (CAA). www.chinaaid.org

China AIDS Orphans Fund (CAOF). www.chinaaidsorphanfund.org

China AIDS Survey. www.casy.org

China Development Brief (CDB). http://chinadevelopmentbrief.com

China HIV/AIDS Information Network (CHAIN). www.homeaids.org

China Information Center. www.observechina.net/info/index.asp

China Internet Network Information Center (CNNIC). www.cnnic.net.cn

China Labor Watch (CLW). www.chinalaborwatch.org

China Labour Bulletin (CLB). www.clb.org.hk

China Monitor. www.chinamonitor.org

China Monthly (magazine). http://minzhuzhongguo.org

Chinarural.org (Carter Center, USA). www.chinarural.org

China Weekly (magazine). http://chinaweekly.com

Citizen Lab. www.citizenlab.org

Committee for Investigation on Persecution of Religion in China (CIPRC). http://china21.org

Committee to Protect Journalists (CPJ). www.cpj.org

Democracy Net. www.asiademo.org

Freenet. www.freenet-china.org

Free Tibet Campaign. www.freetibet.org

Friends of Tibet. www.friendsoftibet.org

Global Ethics Monitor (AFX-GEM). www.globalethicsmonitor.com

Global Voice Online. www.globalvoicesonline.org

Hong Kong Christian Industrial Committee (CIC). www.cic.org.hk

Hong Kong People's Alliance on WTO (HKPAOWTO). www.hkpaowto.org.hk/worldpress

Human Rights First (HRF). www.humanrightsfirst.org

Human Rights in China (HRIC). www.hrichina.org

Human Rights Watch. www.hrw.org

International Campaign for Tibet (ICT). www.savetibet.org

International Center for Human Rights and Democratic Development (ICHRDD). www.echrdd.ca

International Confederation of Free Trade Unions (ICFTU). www.icftu.org

International Federation of Human Rights (FIDH). www.fidh.org

International Labor Organization (ILO). www.ilo.org

International Service for Human Rights (ISHR). www.ishr.ch

Ming Hui Net (Falun Gong Net). www.minghui.org

Minnesota Advocates for Human Rights. www.mnadvocates.org

Reporters without Borders (RSF). www.rsf.org

Students for a Free Tibet (SFT). www.studentsforafreetibet.org

Tibetan Center for Human Rights and Democracy (TCHRD). http://tchrd.org

Tibetan Women's Association (TWA). www.tibetanwomen.org

Transparency International (TI). www.transparency.org

United Nations Development Program: China (UNDP). www.undp.org.cn

United Nations Global Compact. http://unglobalcompact.org

United Nations Office of the High Commissioner of Human Rights (OHCHR). www.unhchr.ch

United Nations Population Fund (UNFPA). www.unfpa.org

U.S. Congressional Executive Commission on China (CECC). www.cecc.gov

Index

About the Author

Xiaobing Li is professor and chair of the Department of History and Geography and director of the Western Pacific Institute at the University of Central Oklahoma. He is the editor of the *American Review of China Studies* and *Western Pacific Journal.* He is also the author or coauthor of the recent books *China at War: An Encyclopedia* (2011), *Voices from the Vietnam War* (2010), *A History of the Modern Chinese Army* (2007), *Taiwan in the 21st Century* (2005), *Voices from the Korean War* (2004), and *Mao's Generals Remember Korea* (2002).